THE COSMIC FAIRY

THE COSMIC FAIRY

THE NEW CHALLENGE OF A DARWINIAN APPROACH TO HUMANISM

Arthur Atkinson B.A.

COLIN SMYTHE LIMITED

First published in Great Britain in 1996
for the Author
by Colin Smythe Limited, Gerrards Cross, Buckinghamshire

British Library Cataloguing in Publication Data

A catalogue record for this book
is available from the British Library

ISBN 0-86140-403-3

The quotations from the poems of A. E. Housman
are reprinted by kind permission of the Society of Authors
as the Literary representatives of the Estate of A. E. Housman

Printed in Great Britain by
Antony Rowe Ltd, Chippenham, Wiltshire

CONTENTS

Humanism. A Foreword by David Bellamy   ix

Preface   xiii

Introduction   xvii

1 *God and the Dinosaurs: our debt to Darwin.*   1
Darwin's theory – absorbed by most religious people and not regarded as a threat to belief – a neglected humanist interpretation of evolution – illustration of its significance – rules out the existence of God.

2 *Emotional Inducements.*   8
Influence of emotional attitudes – clerics, seeing their life-work endangered, oppose atheism as butchers oppose vegetarianism – science and religion co-existed for centuries – now only emotional commitments obscure the clash between them – religion compared with magic.

3 *The Fear of Death.*   13
Man's worst fear – why so many people cling to some religious outlook on life – fears completely removed by humanism – grounds for this claim – the "problem" of suffering – consolations of humanism.

4 *Happiness and Sense Experience.*   18
Satisfaction in the things we actually experience – reliability of our sense organs – misunderstanding of materialism – liberation of thought basic to happiness – no need to search for what exists only in the imagination – overcoming the distress of bereavement – the rewarding merits of our sensations.

5   *Why then, does Religion still Survive?*   24
Little spontaneous interest – impact of past enthusiasm – society
still geared to religious traditions – explanation of the existence of
the universe – language misleading – we survive an accident – in
what sense do we "survive" death?

6   *Morality at Risk.*   29
No necessary connection between good conduct and religion –
in the western world Church long since ceased responsibility
for secular behaviour – morality stems from our culture and
social instincts – is undermined by intolerant religious
convictions.

7   *Civilisation at Risk.*   34
Our philosophy not a religion – the atmosphere of the Middle
Ages – modern humanism entirely secular – nature of Renaissance
Humanism – rediscovery of the works of men – but a deeply
religious deism prevailed – Kenneth Clark's description of
Elizabethan England – Montaigne and Shakespeare – we try to
distinguish between deism and theism – God transcendent, but at
the same time immanent – such bewildering concepts encourage
sectarian and communal disputes – inquisitors and witch-hunters
prosper – civilisation unsafe in the hands of religious people – let
us see that it survives and has come to stay.

8   *Living Together.*   41
What distinctive practical implications follow from humanism? –
rejection of the supernatural in favour of the demanding, but
emotionally fulfilling, experience of human fellowship –
humanism, knowing nothing of national boundaries, offers the
prospect of uniting mankind – religious people just as eager to
promote friendliness and peace – humanists share in their efforts –
but religion is based on an irrational motivation – a dualistic "con"
– a new understanding of human nature provides hope for the
future.

9   *Has Life any Purpose?*   46
No evidence of an intelligent designer of the universe – purpose a
function of thought – must be related to a thinker equipped with a
brain – human purposes pervade our lives – better to concentrate

on directing these to worthwhile ends, rather than attempt to envisage some inscrutable destiny.

10 *Approaching the Question: "Do we have Free Choice?"* 51
Importance of clarity of thought – we seek some light on an issue where philosophers make heavy weather – does humanism, based on the scientific assumption of cause and effect, remove us from all responsibility for our actions? – the problem of determinism remains, but we have a genuine feeling of freedom – the fact that a decision is caused need not affect our sense of its moral value.

11 *Towards a Humanist Psychology.* 57
We have rejected "dualism without", that is, an immaterial world of gods, fairies and spirits – what of "dualism within", an immaterial mind or psyche mysteriously related to a material brain? – also a mistake – a well known philosopher confirms this view.

12 *Disposing of the Mind.* 63
We think with our brains – "the mind" an unnecessary misconception – all uses of the word turn out to refer either to the brain itself or activities of the brain, such as memory – French have no specific word for the mind – the soul, often identified with the mind, can be similarly dismissed.

13 *"People will never change . . ."* 71
Education changes people – our understanding of education – why humanists have a special contribution – the nature of man – children young animals, not young angels – slackening of discipline in the 60's produced parents unable to control their children – need for acceptable discipline – how self-discipline can be encouraged.

14 *Reason and Emotion.* 82
Our needs satisfied, not by the make-believe of religion, but by the warmth of human relationships – the first humanists cultivated reason: we examine the views of some early Greek philosophers – the conflict between reason and emotion – sensitive people value intellectual integrity – demands of religious faith a stressful experience – illustrated by quotations from some Victorian poets

– we conclude with a more recent example, and add a warning about another widespread "con".

15   *The Empty Room.*   92
Some Anglican bishops attempt answers to our question concerning how spirits can communicate with us.

16   *Read it for Yourself.*   101
A new look at the New Testament.

17   *A Cosmic Fairy?*   108
Some scientists appear to believe in one.

18   *Food for Thought.*   113
Some further reflections on Chapters 1 – 17.
We look at additional aspects of the issues we have dealt with in the course of this book.

19   *In Conclusion –*   124
A brief lecture given by the author summarises the philosophy of humanism.

Postscripts   128

Epilogue   136

Index   137

HUMANISM: A FOREWORD

BY DAVID BELLAMY

"Why", the Author asked, "have you agreed to write a Foreword to a book on humanism, when you profess to be a Christian?" "Why", I was tempted to answer, "did you ask me?" However, attached to the letter was a fascinating manuscript; the first I had ever encountered which put the case for humanism uncluttered with rhetoric and contained the challenge of "conversion".

I was brought up in a Baptist family, my father was a respected lay preacher and my mother ran the Sunday School. So I was steeped in the dogma and enjoyed the communion of a working church. I reached my teens with no sign of a road to Damascus even on the horizon and was worried. Dad did his best to cheer me up by admitting that, as a scientist, a pharmacist to be exact, he too fostered doubts about creation or evolution, and had come down on the side of both.

I didn't understand at the time, but the end of the war allowed me to cycle out of the concrete of the suburbs to come face to face with the living countryside. People-made and people-managed it may have been, but it overflowed with biodiversity: the "All things bright and beautiful" products of what I now call creative evolution, the study and conservation of which has fulfilled my life and my faith ever since.

So I make no apologies for the fact that this Foreword is a blatant defence of my position. I wanted new evidence. Perhaps, deep down, I was hoping for conversion. However, the more I read, the more it appeared that the case still revolves around the concept of the noble savage and people's inhumanity to people.

There have, and I trust always will be, noble people, whether primitives (although sadly there are fewer and fewer left every day) or the elite of the twenty-first century. I use the term "people" not simply for gender correctness, but because my Doctorate of Philosophy *in philo sophia* signifies the love of the Goddess of Wisdom.

Wisdom, if not a function, is an amalgam of experience and knowledge. Perhaps pastiche is a better word. For, like life, wisdom is much more than a sum of its parts. One thing it does do (which perhaps sets us aside from all other products of creative evolution) is to give us a free-will choice of good or evil.

It is all too easy to blame man's inhumanity to man or woman on religion: the Wailing Wall, Ulster, all those crusades, the Sacred Grove at Nemi; but it was there in *Homo habilis*, Lucy and the line of primates and vertebrates long before religion took its hold. A hyaena is in competition for the lion's prey and so are the lesser males around the pride. Their wisdom that gains them survival is a sense of place in their pecking order of life. Similarly, when a plant unfolds its leaves, it is in competition with its neighbours (often its offspring) for light, the energy of life itself. Unfriendly competition or submission, the hawk or the dove, sunlight or shade, is the short-term wisdom of survival. A trait that has been passed on ever since nucleic acids coded the information of the selfish gene, the unselfish genes have hung on, programmed for survival as a part of the evolving whole. That is the very essence of creative evolution – the drive towards perfection?

Matter and energy are but two different forms of one and the same thing. That was the original choice. That was the act of creation. Something made it happen. Humanism didn't, because we and it are late arrivals in the arena of change. As a scientist, I don't know what, so I believe in God.

God is my scapegoat and my saviour, giving me the free-will of getting on with the act of living, which, God or no God, is selfish, not selfless.

The book asks "What was God doing before there was man?" Did he see the meanest dinosaur fall? To me the answer must be "Yes". Whether the terrible reptiles visualised God as we do, I have my doubts, but their free-will to stand up and fight or to run away, allowed their gene-set to radiate throughout the world for millions of years, and set both sparrows and our concept of God in motion.

The only thing about this book that really got my hackles up was the idea that spirits have no more credibility than fairies.

"Then why," I had to ask, "wasn't the book entitled The Cosmic Spirit"?

Like God and the Devil, fairies are something some people believe in. They have magical powers to do good or evil. If God or humanism is no more than a good fairy, why didn't he or she, and why don't we, get it right? The spirit of a rugby team, a nation or of God, is something much more relevant; so tangible that it can be felt, driving the whole forward.

The wonderful choice of poetry, a human attribute at its best, almost had me convinced. Tennyson in sombre mood and the "Shropshire Lad" certainly put religiosity in the shade, replacing it with a divine, yet rustic, humanity. But it was Rupert Brooke that pushed me back towards my haven of a belief in God.

> "And in that Heaven of all their wish
> There shall be no more land, say fish."

But then I remembered the old vicarage at Grantchester, a celebration of rural England with all its joys and woes, and realised that the bells that went ting-a-ling and snuffed out Brooke's creative life, were not of a religious war, but one of the inhumanity of pride and power. Likewise those women and children who were hacked to pieces in a church in Rwanda, were victims of race not religion. If in their moments of terminal fear, they felt any comfort from the sanctity of the place, surely that is one reason for believing in God. God gives us a sense of hope, even perhaps, especially in the depths of inhumanity.

Some years ago I was asked to review a book by Konrad Lorenz. It was called *The Waning of Humaneness!* The first half was the best celebration of creative evolution I have ever read. The second half smacked me in the guts, for it said that, by the end of this century, over 60% of the world's population will be living in the urban environment imprinted in concrete. What chance have we then got of making anyone care enough about the living world to try and save it? The only thing that gave me any hope was that it was God's creation he was talking about. Lorenz was an atheist who was evidently losing his faith in humanity, and so I ended my review of his fantastic book with:

> "Goosey goosey gander, wither shall you wander?
> Upstairs and downstairs and in my lady's chamber.
> There I met an old man who wouldn't say his prayers . . ."

Soon after publication he was trying to contact me, and sadly died before I returned his call.

Yes, I suppose I am still muddled up. That is why I decided to write this Foreword; for I knew that if I was going to do a half-decent job, I would have to read it with the care it deserved.

I suppose I did want to be converted, or at least be able, as a human, to believe in my own capabilities; but my road leads me not to suburban Damascus, but to nature's God. The trouble is that of all the products of creative evolution, the one organism of which I am afraid is the one that is made in God's image.

Having now read the book for a third time, I am faced with a predicament and perhaps an answer: like matter and energy, God and Mammon are but two forms of the same thing. As I find it impossible to believe in myself, for I know my imperfections, I have to believe in The Cosmic Spirit, God, and will continue to work towards the perfection of Heaven, here on earth.

"The Cosmic Fairy" deserves more careful reading, and I am sure I will return to it again and again.

Thank you for giving me the opportunity of reading this book.

PREFACE

Readers may ask why I have used the first person plural. Certainly "we" is not a "royal plural", but merely reflects the familiar way in which we present our thoughts for others to consider. Like most humanists, I have absorbed impressions from my own experience and from that of other people, and my interpretation of them has not resulted in any ideas exclusively my own, as the use of "I" might suggest. Humanists help each other to achieve as much understanding as we can. Unlike many religious people, we discuss our views without acrimony and benefit from sharing them.

These thoughts lead me to express my appreciation of the help and encouragement I have received from my friends at Bradlaugh House, the London headquarters of the British Humanist Movements. Other humanists to whom I am especially grateful include Alan Dobson, for spending many hours entering my manuscript into his computer and putting it on a disc, Con Dietrich, who discussed some of my scientific references and Charles Rudd, who frequently checked over the text.

None of these is responsible for the probable presence of stylistic imperfections and, no doubt, some dubious or inaccurate conclusions. I have expressed the hope that these may be excused if readers gain some understanding of humanism as a philosophy that can transform people's lives, disposing of the myth of a spiritual world and leading to friendship in the world of our real experience.

Unfortunately we are ill-equipped to recognise the benefits of humanism. Religion still pervades our culture and discourages us from thinking (for the truth has been revealed). But think we must. It is our nature to do so, and nothing should be allowed to deter us. I have tried to deal with some ideas that may be thought-provoking to thoughtful people, stressing in particular that what I have termed "The Darwinian Enlightenment" comprises a new approach to human nature, and reveals humanism as a simple philosophy of life, combined with a new understanding of human needs. It can stimulate us to co-operate to achieve a less fragile civilisation.

David Bellamy's Foreword may have caused some surprise. Here is a book on humanism which opens with the words of one who earnestly puts the case for religion.

But I consider this wholly appropriate, because many thoughtful people are still searching for a satisfying belief.

I have stressed the simplicity of humanism, so thinking things out is not beyond our ken. This Foreword will stimulate our thoughts. As I said above, we must think. Not only that, but do our best to avoid cultural or emotional bias. We are naturally most at home in our own culture, but only by thinking of our experiences in the context of our humanity can we achieve any understanding.

I wrote this book unaware of what David Bellamy would say. I met him some years ago at the London Butterfly House in Syon Park, when he opened the Garden for native British butterflies, which I had designed. He is a naturalist dedicated to conservation. I see his work as an expression of humanism: hence my invitation.

There are many ways in which people face up to the mystery of life. David Bellamy has described his own religious approach. For a humanist view, read this book. The two can meet in friendship. In practical endeavours we can work together towards "the perfection of Heaven on earth" (David Bellamy's words), and "to find a way of making life on earth enjoyable for all who live there" (my words in my penultimate paragraph).

But the dangers of religion remain. Two particularly disturb me. Its make-belief has invented the problem of evil. That has no solution. The victims of human tragedies have to wrestle with it. We see the turmoil in the Middle East and elsewhere – stimulated by religion. That, too, seems to have no solution.

Creative Evolution implies some sort of process of creation. But who is the Creator? Are God and nature one and the same? To personalise nature merely leads to supernatural speculation – indeed, to magic. Only a Cosmic Fairy could qualify as the creator of a universe. Incidentally, I say "Fairy", not "Spirit". Fairies are beyond our belief. Spirits would fare no better.

Nowadays many religious thinkers are trying to rationalise the concept of God. This is nothing new in theology. But has it ever worked? Do we really experience any "spiritual" world? Is it not far better to accept the mystery of our existence? The natural world is fascinating, even if we cannot completely comprehend how it came about. Why invent a supernatural one?

THIS BOOK WILL PRESENT THE CHALLENGE OF HUMANISM.

I dedicate it to my wife, Pamela.

INTRODUCTION

To whom are we addressing this book: to anyone who is interested in humanism and seeks information?

Ours is a more clearly defined audience than this. We think of many members of the lay public – thoughtful people, seeking a satisfying attitude to life. Included are numbers who are knowledgeable in many respects, but, not having any specialised historical or philosophical training, are at a disadvantage when called upon to choose between, or criticise, the pronouncements of those who regard themselves as qualified to guide us on religious matters.

This book is intended to be read by such, and its aim is largely twofold: to dispute the idea that we have a genuine religious experience, and to affirm quite simply that we live in one world, that is, the world of people, places and material things, which we really do experience. This real world removes the anxieties and fears which a belief in an imaginary world engenders. No "Cosmic Fairy" presides over our existence.

Ever since the beginnings of social organisation rulers have sought to control their subjects by the sanctions of an otherworldly being. We now suggest that society needs a sounder basis for morality, because modern knowledge cannot be reconciled with myths. We see in humanism the most appropriate response to the problems which life poses. We deceive ourselves if we think that a sense of wonder and mystery need have anything to do with religion, or that religion can answer our questions. Humanism does not offer any complete solutions, but provides a way of thinking rationally and scientifically, which gives us enough to be going on with and shows us the way towards a satisfying life. It is, indeed, a recipe for happiness.

Man struggles against man and confronts the forces of nature at the same time. Famines, floods and the like have never received his undivided attention. There was some excuse for this in times of scarcity, but now that technical efficiency has placed ample resources at man's disposal – provided birth control becomes effective – he has the opportunity to take charge of his own development. The struggle against nature can be replaced by co-operation, for many of its forces can be readily harnessed.

But man must cease hostility to man, and unfortunately, religion fuels the flames of discord. Isaiah's vision sounds admirable:"... and they shall beat their swords into ploughshares, and their spears into pruning hooks; nation shall not lift up sword against nation, neither shall they learn war any more". All, however, is conditional. Nations are required to ascend "the mountain of the Lord" and wait upon "the house of the God of Jacob," and " out of Zion shall go forth the law". Of course, as history so clearly shows, nations are not prepared to forsake their own exclusive "holy mountains", which demand their unswerving loyalty and devotion. The very land where Isaiah's feet once trod – the "Holy Land" – has presented a sorry spectacle for those who think that religion promotes peace.

Humanism invites us to face real situations, not imaginary ones. What these realities are and how best we should deal with them, will, we hope, become clearer during the course of this book; but, to suggest a definition of humanism in a few words, we would say that it is concerned with the nature of living organisms. All life is natural and has evolved by natural causes without any supernatural affiliations. Primitive man attained consciousness, not only of the world about him, but of himself and his own thought processes. But language and conceptual thought have not only resulted in science. Dreams and misinterpretation of natural phenomena led primitive man to devise an inner world of supernatural entities, which he projected on to nature, unaware of the potency of his vivid imagination.

Humanism eliminates the so-called supernatural, and leaves man no option but to co-operate with his fellow men. Only thus can human needs be discovered and their satisfaction achieved. But understanding and friendship can be disastrously inhibited or completely submerged by religious passions, which wreck harmonious living in the pursuit of vain imaginings. We hope to show that common sense merits more consideration than is normally conceded by the experts, emotionally committed, as most of them are, to traditional doctrines on which their professional status depends.

Indeed, we have throughout laid emphasis on people's intelligence but we need to include a warning. In science the satisfactory understanding of the complexities of cosmology, mathematics, biochemistry, molecular biology, not to mention quantum mechanics, brings us to areas far removed from normal experience. We shall have more to say about this when, after our closing chapter, we recommend, among books for further reading, *The Unnatural Nature of Science*, by Lewis Wolpert (Faber and Faber, 1992).

Briefly, our reply is to point out that these difficulties, although a challenge to human intelligence, are not essential to the happiness of mankind. Many problems of human relationships are simple if freed from religious assumptions.

It will not be easy to maintain a high level of quality writing throughout this book. But in a discursive survey of humanism, we suggest that readers may be stimulated by some new (or neglected) aspects of the subject. These include a demonstration of the non-existence of God (Chapter 1), the removal of the fear of death (Chapter 3), a new approach to psychology (Chapters 11 and 12) and the role of humanism in education (Chapter 13).

We try to uncover a few nuggets of greater value than the rest of the material, much of which, no doubt, suffers from various verbal and factual deficiencies. For these we ask our readers' indulgence, because this rational, scientific and emotionally satisfying view of life, replacing the make-belief of religion, is a vital necessity if Planet Earth is to retain a liveable environment. Up to now there has been little recognition of our responsibility to each other within the context of a world-wide community. Pollution and the thoughtless destruction of the animate and inanimate assets necessary for the survival of living things have increasingly endangered the prospects of our own and other species.

All those who suspect that priests and other proponents of the supernatural are, however unintentionally, misleading us, should have patience and read on. Here is something that people *can* believe in.

We need to wake up to the fact that mankind is suffering from an affliction that has dogged the human race throughout history. It can, we suggest, be best described as a misunderstanding of human nature, and religion has played a major role in its continuing survival.

A humanist re-interpretation of human nature will reveal that our animal instincts – the "wolf in man" – are not implanted in us by the devil, as some religious people have supposed. Consider all the myths about werewolves. Such myths refer to a natural stage in the process that has led from animal life to civilisation. An over-simplification? Perhaps, but the general development is clear enough. Civilisation can win through. Of course, if Utopia lies ahead, we shall not see it ourselves; but herein consists one of the challenges of humanism. Our developing social instincts prompt us to take part in the struggle and by doing so feel at home in the world. An exposition of this view will be found during the course of the following pages.

The key to our new understanding is a determination to think without cultural or emotional bias. In other words, we need to be honest in our thoughts and be content with what we actually experience. Incidentally, let feminists realise that "Honest to Man" means also honest to women. "Man" in this sense is cognate with the Latin word, *homo*, which means a human being. "Homo est", said Atticus in a letter to his friend, Cicero, whom he wished to console on the death of the latter's daughter, Tullia. "She is human". And here, indeed, is the simple idea that pervades this book. We are human and must accept the mystery of existence in this context. Mere senseless mystification will result if we invent another world endowing us with super-human affiliations. Only our imagination will make fantasy real.

It will not take long to read this short book, and we hope readers will be moved to join a humanist organisation and find satisfaction in helping to make the world a pleasant home for humanity, not forgetting other sentient beings.

Let our species prosper. We stand a better chance than the dinosaurs. A degree of intelligence which had not evolved in their days, is available to us. If we use it, the following equation could be realised:

Technology + birth-control + friendship = a pleasant future for the human race.

ONE

GOD AND THE DINOSAURS: OUR DEBT TO DARWIN

*"The Darwinian Enlightenment" has introduced a new
understanding of nature and of ourselves: an entirely natural
conception of both.*

Evolution so disturbed the Victorians because they saw it as undermining the biblical account of creation, but after the initial shock, most thoughtful Christians absorbed the impact and reluctantly came to terms with it. Sheer intellectual necessity forced clerical defenders of the faith to retreat from untenable defences. The new ideas were skilfully reconciled with the old, and after the dust had settled, they were no longer regarded as a threat to religion. Darwin had merely clarified the method God used to produce this wonderful world. Even the time scale ceased to be a problem. In fact, the Bible had not got it entirely wrong. We were just mistaken to suppose that God had overworked himself. Could not the "days" of creation be symbolic for vast periods of time?

But can the damage to traditional belief be so easily repaired?

It is suggested that Darwin himself was a worried Darwinian and kept a low profile for a number of years. Not he but Huxley most effectively popularised evolution. We now contend that humanism has something fresh to say. Religious people face a more serious collision between faith and biological science than was previously suspected. We do not refer to the findings of neo-Darwinism, that is, the genetic bases of variation in living organisms – knowledge made possible by Mendel and unknown to Darwin. It is certain implications of the evolutionary process itself that have been largely overlooked or neglected, but do actually demolish the foundations of supernatural belief. Religious fundamentalists have always suspected this and

1

maintain a widespread rearguard action. But sympathetic humanists have been loath to accept the admission. For we cannot ignore the distressing effect of atheism on committed believers, and many critics of religion, having been brought up in the faith, well appreciate its emotional vitality. So we are ourselves strongly motivated to support the intellectual justification for a belief in God, conceding that his existence cannot be disproved.

It would, indeed, alleviate much anxiety if this attitude could be sustained, but the time has come to reassess the implications of evolution and point out that it provides weighty evidence which enables us to express the view that the non-existence of God can, indeed, be conclusively demonstrated.

What do we mean by proof? We have just used the word "demonstrated". Is this the same thing? Anyway, as all human knowledge is provisional, would not agnosticism be more appropriate? No. We shall discuss this in relation to fairies. We are not concerned about proving their non-existence, as most people are satisfied that we can demonstrate it, and do not worry further. Nor do we feel the need to raise doubts for schoolboy mathematicians when they so confidently conclude the Euclidean propositions with Q.E.D.

Claiming, then, that our demonstration puts on the whole mantle of proof, we shall invite readers to explore a neglected feature of evolution which renders any concept of God impossible. In stressing the simplicity of our explanation, we anticipate efforts to discredit what to us is an obvious conclusion. Our opponents will want to know why, if all is so clearly perceptible, learned scholars still maintain that evolution, if not a friend to religion, is far from hostile to it, and will further attempt to mislead people. We shall, of course, try to deal later with such criticism which is levelled at humanism in general and point out the emotional and cultural factors involved. Now however, we have a new situation. Religious controversy has been going on for many hundreds of years, and during all this time it has not been difficult for those in authority to deal with criticism and render the dispute intellectually acceptable. But evolution has entered the field comparatively recently, so it is not surprising that certain of its implications have been too hastily brushed aside, encouraging us to assume that a truce has been agreed and further hostilities are unnecessary. This is far from the case, as we hope soon to demonstrate.

Our reasoning will centre round two key words: consciousness and intelligence. But first let us prepare the way for an imaginative experience that will provide a realistic background and help to illustrate our contention.

To set the scene we need to remind ourselves that God is generally regarded as active in the world. He is intimately involved with people, answering their prayers and inspiring devotion. He is a real entity with personal attributes. So no objection should be raised to our supposing that religious people would consider God to be just as real and diligent before there were any humans on the earth, and we should not be accused of asking a frivolous question if we want to know how he spent his time before we absorbed so much of his attention.

Thanks to the revelations made known to us as post-Darwinians, we have an idea of what some former earthlings were doing before we appeared. So let us consider a really noteworthy episode in the development of pre-human life on earth. We choose it because the spectacular nature of the scene will add vividness to the point we shall try to make, but our imagination will not lead us too far astray because the records are firmly imprinted in the rocks.

We refer to the age of the dinosaurs. It was an outstanding period and, at least in western countries, has been made very popular in books both for adults and children. So there is no need to paint a picture of these amazing animals. We are all familiar not only with their size and other anatomical extravagances, but with their diversity and world-wide distribution. Above all we are impressed by the duration of their dominance, lasting many millions of years and far surpassing the brief spell enjoyed up to now by recognisable humans.

The Garden of Eden, we are told, began in perfection. That would have had no meaning in the world of the dinosaurs, none, that is to say, if we ascribe our moral values to them. A fierce and ruthless free-for-all was the order of the day, and perfection would be measured in terms of survival value.

But what was God's attitude to all this, as his presence in these times was no less a reality? Perhaps he was not interested, as the dinosaurs had no religion, for they had no speech. God could not communicate with them. (Incidentally, a theological problem seems to arise here. When God contemplated the dinosaurs, in what language did he express his thoughts? Today he has a wide choice, but presumably he was not speechless before the advent of human speech. We are glad to leave this problem with the theologians.)

Perhaps we may suppose that God did not expect too much of the dinosaurs, because the evolution of desirable social conduct, initiated by him, had hardly got under way. After all, they may have displayed some rudiments of it if they showed concern for their young ones, as their near descendants, the crocodiles, have been observed to do. God's omniscience and foreknowledge would be relevant here, and we must not forget to include patience among the divine virtues.

Leaving a light-hearted speculation, (for which we offer no apology, as it follows directly from the anthropomorphic view of God, which cannot be avoided if he is to be credited with activity in the world), we now draw attention to the first of our key words. The dinosaurs did not advance to civilised behaviour, but they did achieve a high level of consciousness, and it is the evolution of consciousness that needs to be examined. Once more we stress that a complex topic can be dealt with simply.

Consciousness came along with the development of animal nervous systems, and we can trace its progress from the earliest animal organisms. Invertebrates are aware of their environment and interact with it, but the full potential of consciousness emerged most clearly when the vertebrates acquired more effective limbs and other organs that could explore the world. It is a function of animal nervous systems and reached its peak in mammalian brains, when what we experience as self-consciousness evolved. The dinosaurs were conscious of themselves, of course, but lacking language, could not know that they were dinosaurs.

And now consider intelligence. We make no attempt to define it, but clearly it depends on consciousness (which we have also left undefined.) The point we wish to emphasis – the whole *raison d'être* of this chapter – is that intelligence has evolved along with consciousness, and is a property of animal brains, pre-eminently some human ones. (The dinosaurs are thought to have made a poor showing in this respect.) There is no justification whatever for assuming it and applying it to any other entities. That is not to say that intelligence could not have evolved elsewhere in the universe, but it would need some organism equipped with some mental (=brain) system to manifest it. We certainly cannot assign it to God and at the same time regard him as prior to the evolutionary process in which it developed.

The reason should now have become obvious why we cannot accept the existence of God. Intelligence came on stage late in the evolutionary drama. It did not raise the curtain. But of all the qualities attributed to God, intelligence would surely be a prime necessity. So among our conjectures concerning the beginning of things, we cannot include the presence of God. Without intelligence no active agent could possibly make sense. Incidentally, we have dealt only with intelligence, but the same argument would apply to all the emotional and other human qualities attributed to God. Were he to be supplied with a body, that too would meet with the same objection. Of course religious thinkers realise that God cannot have a physical body, and accordingly assign him a "spiritual" one. "God is a spirit", we read in St. John's Gospel. But spirits are no more credible than fairies.

So we are left with the humanist view that we should accept the mystery of existence and not attempt to "solve" it by inventing a further mystery.

Perhaps we should ask "Why bother?" God comforts and inspires so many people. Does it matter that he does not exist and that their faith is based on an unreal world of their own imagination? We think it does for reasons that later chapters will explain.

And just a comment on the levity of parts of this chapter which some may find offensive. The incredibility of religious belief needs to be brought home to those who quote its benefits. Humanism offers an alternative to make-believe to console the distressed; and as for the faith that inspires good works, it is a kind-hearted attitude that really prompts them. We do not have to be religious to do good.

Here we have come to grips straightaway with the basic claim of humanism, namely, that we live in one world – a natural world without a divine presence. We shall now go on to consider other aspects which reveal it as a simple philosophy of life, yet able to inspire and fortify human endeavours.

Of course, it may occur to discerning people who have followed our reasoning so far that further discussion is pointless. If there is no God, nothing more needs to be said, as the very ground of religious conviction has been undermined. Humanism, however, involves so much more than disbelief. It is a positive, and, as we have just said, inspirational attitude to life. Our succeeding chapters should make this clear and we shall begin by seeking to expose the emotional claims of religion and show that we need not be misled by the self-appointed advocates of various religious systems. Our approach will avoid the complicated thinking indulged in by so many philosophers and theologians, who stir up such a cloud of unnecessary obscurities that they block the view and no one can see ahead. But first we need to realise that belief in God is no mere innocent delusion. We are mistaken if we suppose that we can embrace it harmlessly just to be on the safe side. The seventeenth century French philosopher, Blaise Pascal, thought this and proposed his famous wager. Thinking people, he said, should believe in God because, if they disbelieve and he exists, they are in real trouble, but if they believe and he does not exist, they have had nothing to lose. So hedge your bet and settle for God's existence. This is misleading advice, for on the other hand, there is very much to gain from unbelief. We shall have more to say on this later. Let us now note just one of the merits of a humanist view. Disposing of God enables us to get rid of the Devil, who was invented along with God, and the intractable problem of how a good and all-powerful God can countenance evil vanishes too. Gone is the tension that pervades the lives of thinking religious people, and no longer need vast resources be wasted on building shrines, temples, cathedrals, mosques and pyramids, all sadly based on an illusion.

Meanwhile, humanism clearly points the way towards a satisfying life. It even removes the fear of death and frees our thoughts for dealing with the urgent demands of living. There is fairly general agreement that the environment is now facing dangers which threaten the very habitability of the planet, and it seems reasonable to suggest that we are unlikely to be able to cope with these unless new thinking is brought to bear. Humanism makes this possible. Freeing us from religious constraints, it opens up the way to a better understanding of both ourselves and our behaviour. We shall try to justify this claim in the following pages when we deal with psychology and consider the new insight that humanism offers to education.

Above all we shall seek to refute the credibility of a "spiritual" designer of the universe. This chapter shows how Darwin has enlightened us in a way that is as yet hardly appreciated. It is time we realised that a "being" without physical properties cannot partake of functions that have developed over the course of evolution. A "Cosmic Fairy" is no solution to the mystery of existence.

TWO

EMOTIONAL INDUCEMENTS

Traditional attitudes find expression in religion,
which stirs up and relies upon deeply embedded emotions.

Life can be very confusing. We all want to have some understanding of its problems, but few possess the time or the ability to acquire the specialised knowledge necessary to follow the opinions of the experts. In fact, the vast mass of expertise in all fields of knowledge seems to give good reason to suppose that most people's views are almost worthless.

However, two considerations may suggest that expert opinion in certain important subjects is not always reliable. Firstly, more is involved in forming an opinion than knowledge and brain-power, the additional factor being a person's emotional attitude. Secondly, experts often differ quite fundamentally among themselves.

Nowhere are the experts more subjected to emotional influences than in religion. The severity of the pressure is seldom admitted, but it can be seen to be overwhelming when examined. Most ministers of Christianity, for example, are sincere, benevolent and dedicated people, and although they claim to place the service of God before that of man, they do in practice measure the former in terms of the latter, and dedicate their lives to human welfare. So when the radical claims of humanism threaten their life-work, a most formidable emotional barrier comes into play. Such is its strength that they have little difficulty in preserving intellectual integrity by the skilful use of arguments. Moreover, when reason proves to be inadequate, committed believers have a trump card marked "faith". And faith is, indeed, as the writer of the Epistle to the Hebrews so aptly described it, the assurance of things hoped for, the evidence of things not seen.

As for differences between expert opinions, the field of religion provides an embarrassing number of examples. Clearly the conflicting doctrines of various religions cannot all be true. Christianity, in particular, fails to escape intact. Some theologians maintain that the Incarnation, miracles and Resurrection are myths, and urge a form of Christianity in which these myths are discarded. But it seems hardly possible to reconcile such opinions with those that are still widely supported by other experts as orthodox Christian beliefs. And when it comes to defining the nature of God, exceedingly divergent views compete. These, incidentally, sometimes appear to be compatible only because of the obscurity of their phrasing.

The point concerning emotion is especially important because we shall stress that humanism is really a very simple outlook on life, and, feelings apart, can be understood by people not necessarily equipped with more than average intelligence. This claim, of course, invites the question "If humanism is so simple and obvious, why is it so little known and understood?" We must also ask whether humanists themselves are exposed to emotional influences.

To deal first with the second question, of course all people respond to emotional influences to some extent, and we are far from wishing to remove emotion from human life. So vital is it, that we will pause briefly and try to define the term. Perhaps we should consider first a word we used above, namely, "feeling". It is closely associated with emotion, but has two quite distinct meanings, which are liable to be confused. We feel the presence of an object by touching it, or we feel pain or pleasure in a limb. But we also "feel" love, hate, affection, dislike, security, uneasiness, gratitude, ungratefulness and so forth. These "feelings" are usually called emotions, and it is necessary to realise that, whereas "feeling" when caused by external or internal bodily sensations, is largely objective and not wholly under our control, "feelings" like love or anger are subjective processes of thought, and can be modified if we summon up the power to do so. Such emotions frequently result in experiences of pleasure or pain, and so enrich or disrupt our lives. But we must beware lest they take over and cloud our judgement. This means that we should make an honest effort to recognise the emotional bases of religious beliefs. Perhaps they are held on account of tradition, a sense of comfort, loyalty or even the vague assertion that many people make when faced with the apparently inexplicable mystery of existence: " Well . . . . There must be something . . . !"

Although humanists stand a better chance of avoiding injurious emotions than religious people, they must still stress the need to make a great effort to be honest to themselves and others. After all, being "honest to God" is of no great consequence – for who supposes that a god would be likely to be deceived? We can, however, easily mislead ourselves and others by not thoroughly thinking out all sides of a question, or by allowing emotions too much control over our reason. Incidentally, it is desirable to confine ourselves to the examination of our own honesty, and not freely imply that others are dishonest. If a bishop decries atheism, or a butcher opposes vegetarianism, obviously they have an axe to grind, but we must suppose that they honestly believe it to be a very worthy axe. All we have suggested is that emotional factors should not be discounted, pointing out that they are rarely given the attention their intensity demands.

Coming next to the simplicity of humanism, its nature will, of course, be discussed in ensuing pages, but what we have said about emotion provides a clue to the limited acceptance of the obvious. If we claim simplicity for a view of life, some will say that we misinterpret our experience, and that life is not so simple as people imagine. (To this we answer briefly that many aspects of life, especially scientific concepts, are indeed difficult to understand, but that certain important ones – on which our happiness may very well depend – are made to look needlessly involved.) For many, seeing that humanism involves disbelief in religion, will "feel" that it must be wrong, and use their intelligence to find reasons for retaining a system of belief that leaves room for religion.

We now have to apply to humanists the criticism levelled earlier at religious people, namely, that their views are divided and conflicting. Frequently coupled with this is the complaint that humanism is too negative. Religion is denied, but what is put in its place? We will, however, refer to the first of these criticisms, as the positive side of the humanist outlook will be dealt with later.

Humanism is an attitude to life and not a set of beliefs, so that the differences of opinion, apart from this attitude, need not be damaging to the humanist movement. Attitudes do not, of course, arise without certain assumptions, and there is an assumption shared by all humanists: man has evolved through natural processes, and must come to terms with the rest of nature, without expecting supernatural assistance. This is, however, not so much an assumption about the nature of the world, as one suggesting the method man should employ to meet the challenge of his environment, that is, to rely on his own resources. Similarly, scientists do not take knowledge for granted, but only the validity of the experimental method. Magicians, on the other hand, assume knowledge: we can manipulate nature because we have the right formulae. This is not unlike a religious attitude, according to which the faithful believe that the course of their lives can be influenced by supernatural intervention. It is not quite the same, because whereas magic usually seems to work automatically, prayer always depends upon the will of a supposed conscious heavenly agent. But it is easy to assume that God is available to help those who have found the necessary relationship with him or approach him in the correct manner. (Practically any member of any religious sect will gladly dispel the ignorance of anyone who seeks to be put on the right path.) Here, as with magic, we need to possess accurate information, and where knowledge is of prime importance, conflicting and contradictory ideas become a serious liability.

We may say that religious people try to attain indisputable truth; in fact, they frequently claim to possess it. "You shall know the truth, and the truth shall make you free." Whereas, scientists seek to discover as many true statements as possible, but even these are provisional, for further research may invalidate them. Humanists share this enquiring attitude, and are not to be confused with religious people, who rather resemble magicians in their approach to nature.

A glance at the historical background will show how a further confusion can easily arise between science itself and the scientific attitude. The one should imply the other, but it need not do so, for science can be studied uncritically. Some Christians would persuade us that during and for some time after the Renaissance there was no clash between science and religion, because most scientists of that period were members of the Church. They point out that Roger Bacon wrote a book, at the request of the Pope, to show that the new learning supported the Christian faith. For some time, indeed, the conflict between the attitudes of science and religion was not generally appreciated. It was, of course, easy, especially in the Middle Ages, when the sum total of knowledge was less, for a brilliant brain, such as Leonardo da Vinci's, to encompass most of it, and still remain within the fold of the Christian tradition. And even as late as the founding of the Royal Society in 1662, the majority of leading scientists were Christians. Sir Isaac Newton regarded his theological speculations as no less important than his scientific ones. But as knowledge increased, the need to specialise resulted in a quickening of the critical approach to science, and when, in the field of biology, Darwin produced his *Origin of Species*, Bishop Wilberforce realised that this and the biblical account of creation were incompatible. The two represented conflicting attitudes, and these persist today, in spite of a massive withdrawal by progressive members of the Church from some of its dogmatic positions. The over-emotional reaction of many religious people still clouds their vision, and causes them to misinterpret the significance of the experiences that life provides.

How sad it is that, whereas everyone knows quite well what magicians are doing when they make real things vanish, religious people are so easily deluded when told that things that are not there are real.

A religious attitude is so deeply embedded in our culture, that our emotions tempt us to refrain from criticising it when the discoveries of science should lead us to do so.

THREE

THE FEAR OF DEATH

An unnecessary fear.

Many people are content to ignore the mystery of life and pursue the absorbing pastime of living, leaving to the experts the burden of thinking things out. Let the scientists answer the question "How?" and the priesthood the question "Why?" Even when the latter proffer a "simple faith", their assumptions raise daunting complexities that discourage too many questions.

Our aim is to change all this, for we propose that, although existence is a mystery, the simple aspects – and we shall deal only with these – of many involved subjects are both vital to human welfare and well within the range of normal intelligence. Moreover, we plan to introduce some considerations which, if not new, have been surprisingly disregarded by the professionals.

So we are not producing a systematic treatise on humanism, but some relevant lines of thought that will, we hope, build up and illuminate the humanist outlook. Nor should readers expect a faultless presentation or a set of watertight arguments. We should be foolish to suppose that we can attain more than a measure of understanding of ourselves and the world. Our theme is that humanism offers the most satisfactory philosophy of life.

Let us, then, consider next a further cause of its unpopularity and suggest another reason why so many people, if pressed, cling to some sort of religious outlook on life.

The circumstances are rather strange. Religion itself is far from enjoying the widespread popularity that its supporters desire. Closed or half-empty churches are witness to this fact. Nor do people talk much about religion. Even clergymen tend to avoid the subject, and are far more inclined to ask about one's health or discuss the weather. It is evident that most people most of the time can manage quite nicely without religion; but there are exceptions, namely, the crucial events of human life, such as those related to birth, marriage and death. These are commonly occasions when priests are called in and traditional religious ceremonies take over.

In our view the last of these events presents a serious stumbling block in the way of the acceptance of humanism. The fear of death is probably man's worst fear, and could he but get rid of it, the most painful of human apprehensions would disappear. It has dogged his consciousness since the early stages of human development and is, in fact, a penalty of increased self-consciousness. Animals do not seem to be aware that life will end, but there came a time when primitive man realised this and could not bring himself to face it, a reluctance which has remained with us ever since. But in early times it was easier to escape into fantasy. Being ignorant of the causes of natural phenomena such as storms and rainbows, man allowed his imagination to invent a world of gods and spirits, who were responsible for natural forces; and, having no mortal bodies, were not subject to death. We can only surmise such human reactions in their very early stages. Perhaps people encountered these spirits in their dreams and, not being restrained by the demands of scientific realism, transferred them to the world outside. Children need little encouragement to appreciate fairy stories, but they are expected to grow out of them.

The religious, then, or more specifically, the Christian answer when faced with death is well known. It is the gateway to another life. People do not really die – only their bodies. Their "souls" or "spirits" continue to live. In some mysterious sense there is life after death. The trouble is, of course, that nobody has the slightest idea what this means. Even committed believers confess to times of distressing doubt. Were it not for the horror that most people have of death, few could sustain a belief in such an ill-defined future life in face of the reality of the termination of the present one. Let us make no mistake. Most people can live with the prospect of death only because it is so seldom mentioned, and when it can be no longer ignored, euphemisms abound. An expression such as "passed on" is preferable to describing the stark facts.

In actuality, of course, the finality of death is fully recognised, as is indicated by the prevalence of the saying "We only live once", and, although no one stands up to contradict the clergy at funeral services, affirmations about reunions in the hereafter provide no permanent satisfaction. People choose just to bury their heads in the sand. But is it not a matter of vital concern – this question that is so studiously avoided? If we really do live for ever, surely here is something about which we should not be ill-informed. To be left in suspense, and told that heaven can be known only by faith, may lead to the stress of painful unbelief.

In contrast to the disturbing influence of religion, humanism completely removes the fear of death. We make no attempt to deny its reality, but merely draw attention to a fact that is so obvious that it is generally overlooked: death can never be experienced. We cannot "be" dead. Only life can be experienced. How, then, can we form any emotional attitude towards a state that we shall never know? It is worth dwelling on this view for a moment, as its revealing clarity needs getting used to, and we search in vain for any discussion of it among the professional providers of consolation.

Traditionally most exponents of religious ideas are reticent and vague about what occurs in life after death, but others are more explicit, quite regardless of the misleading language they use. We can speak sensibly of our experiences when we are alive, and because of this we tend to assume that it makes equal sense to speak of what may happen to us when "we are" dead. Most certainly we have nothing to fear, for we shall not be there. We did not exist before our appearance in this world, and, in a manner of speaking, we were not heard to complain about it. So why should we fear non-existence in the future? Extinction would be a formidable prospect only if we could experience it.

Reflections such as these help us to face up to the unpleasant things that frequently cause death, such as violence, accidents and disease. All these are hazards of life. Death itself should bring no apprehension. In fact the biological necessity of death is obvious if we pause to consider. Without it life would be impossible. Animals need to feed on each other and the earth's resources would become exhausted if living organisms lived forever.

Of course removing the fear of death does nothing to dispel the sorrow experienced in the loss of loved and valued friends and relatives who have died, but the Christian claim that we shall all meet again is attractive only to those who are prepared to give no further thought to the matter. Any measure of understanding is out of the question. We can understand only one meaning for life, and that has an earthly context. Any other meaning is a product of our imagination. Humanists realise this, and further that we do not need to escape the consequences of death for the simple reason that, as we have explained, it does not concern us. What we do escape are the groundless fears and anxieties that go with pretence and wishful thinking.

Humanists, taking a natural rather than a supernatural view of man, do not believe that all sorrow can be removed from human life, and their answer to its impact is not to rely on divine consolation, but by mutual sympathy, kindness and understanding, so to heighten the quality of our friendship with one another, that grief can be relieved by the warmth of social concern. We know that life is full of pain and disaster. Diseases, hurricanes and earthquakes, to say nothing of the frequently unpleasant experiences involved in dying, are an inevitable part of human life, but, if we exercise the capacities of our human nature, we have the resources to overcome them. Here humanism apprehends an understanding vastly superior to the perplexity of religion. Religious thinkers wonder why there should be so much undeserved suffering. Why should a benevolent and all-powerful God allow good and kind people to suffer through no fault of their own? But this "problem" of suffering is their own invention and does not exist for humanists. For us the problem is not how to account for suffering, but how best to relieve it, and, as we have indicated, this is a matter for mutual assistance.

Most systems of religious belief try to establish the reality of things that are real only to the imagination, and so give rise to predictable conflicts in people's thinking. Such contradictions in thought easily undermine mental stability and lead to numerous forms of religious enthusiasms and neuroses with which we are all too familiar. Christians, for example, claim that their religion is a source of joy and comfort, but at the same time allow the central symbol of their faith to depict agony and humiliation. Again, many give all they have to the relief of suffering, yet some actually go out of their way to suffer, and deliberately lead lives of austerity, deprivation and hardship. In fact, holiness can become associated with the denial of "earthly" pleasures. The very fact that humanism stands unequivocally for the enjoyment of life makes it suspect in their eyes. But what a relief it is to shed this offensive attitude which makes a virtue of misery, and to recognise the virtue of happiness. To none is life available for freehold: to all on lease. Let us make good use of it while we have it. Its quality is of our own making.

Indeed it is an outstanding merit of the humanist outlook that it helps people to avoid the agonizing efforts required of those who try to interpret personal or social disasters in terms of a divine dispensation. Frequently we meet unhappy sufferers who insist that their troubles must be part of God's plan. They do not understand it, but in the end all will be revealed. What tragic experiences they have to endure, imposed on them quite unnecessarily by fictitious religious ideas.

FOUR

HAPPINESS AND SENSE EXPERIENCE

Removal of the stresses caused by religion enhances our
appreciation of life. Our senses delight us.
"What is this life, if, full of care,
We have no time to stand and stare?"

As humanists, then, having relieved ourselves of the fear of death, we are free to enjoy an enhanced quality of life – one in which we can achieve happiness without strings, for we are no longer tied down to beliefs which are a burden on the intellect.

Let us in this chapter reinforce the satisfaction and stimulation which result from the knowledge that we can be honest in our thought. Humanists deal solely with the actual objects revealed by our senses. We do not have to pretend to ourselves or try to persuade ourselves that there is a reality, other than the material world around us, which is inaccessible to our senses. But some philosophers, particularly those with a religious view of life, never tire of adding to people's confusion by insisting on the unreliability of our sense organs. Things are not what they seem. A table only has the appearance of being solid. Actually it is far otherwise, containing more empty space than "solid" matter. This, of course, leaves the field wide open for the existence of any number of entities that cannot be detected by human senses. So we will take up the contention, avoiding the jargon and technical terms of the experts, and see if we can dispute the point, using ordinary simple language.

True, a table is revealed as vastly different when examined with the aid of scientific instruments, but we would have no knowledge of this were it not for our senses. Our sense organs may not be perfectly accurate, and unable of themselves to provide a complete description of an object, but they are all we have to keep us in contact with the world outside us. If there was any reality in our environment beyond the scope of our senses, we could not possibly know anything about it – just as we can know nothing about objects in outer space that are inaccessible to our instruments, the latter being, of course, extensions of our sense organs. Through experience, our brains have acquired the ability to interpret our sensations, so that, although a straight stick looks bent when viewed through water, we know from our knowledge of the behaviour of light in water, that it is actually straight. Thus, our senses do a reasonably good job, and in cases where they are inadequate, we have our instruments and our experience to help them. There appears to be no reliable evidence of any other means by which we become aware of things and events outside ourselves. Certainly "mediums" claim to make contact with "spiritual" entities, that is, "dead" people who have passed over to the "other side"; but nowadays very few philosophers or scientists take them seriously. In any case, those who attend spiritualist seances are invited to experience the alleged manifestations with their senses. There does not seem to be any extra-sensory perception involved.

The more we study a materialistic view of life, the more satisfying and sensible it seems. But we cannot ignore the carefully fostered horror of materialism that is prevalent no less in the press and on radio and television, than in the pulpit. In many a discussion the comment "This is sheer (or rank, crass, stark, or sordid) materialism!" is enough to end the argument. Materialism is generally regarded as cold and lacking in emotional attractiveness. It is usually connected with selfishness and greed. Worst of all, communists are materialists, and look at their ruthless political methods! But before we shudder unduly at this unhappy picture, let us realise that such criticisms can be applied to anyone, and are no more to be aimed specifically at materialists than at some religious people. Indeed, only the more liberal religions encourage toleration and freedom of thought and expression. We do not find these flourishing in countries where dogmatic religion has great influence. In fact, ruthlessness and intolerance have in the past been more characteristic of religion than at the present time, (with certain sad exceptions). This we can easily understand, because then religious people, fervently believing that they had a divine revelation of the truth, also exercised most of the powers that are today in the hands of the secular authorities. The less dogmatic views of most modern Christians represent a movement away from a typically religious attitude – views, we may note, which have been forced upon them by people's clearer understanding of themselves and their environment.

How easy it is to give way to prejudice and accept conventional ideas thoughtlessly! Far from being harsh, the atmosphere of materialism is likely to be warm and friendly, for it is concerned with flesh and blood – people and human companionship. Although God may seem to be present for believers "when two or three are gathered together," on the whole a mystical approach to life tends to isolate individuals: "But thou, when thou prayest, enter into thy closet, and when thou hast shut the door, pray to thy Father. . . ." Although worship may be public, the vital process of consulting their God is best performed by believers in private. We observe, however, that most Christian people do not attach much emphasis to this, but busily organise church socials because they feel instinctively the need for fellowship.

The intellectual gift which we receive from humanism, that is, freedom from the necessity of chasing phantoms, will irritate many professional philosophers. They will not encourage the contentment we derive from a philosophy of common-sense. We shall be accused of triviality and of dismissing important objections in a few sentences. But we need not be deterred by their disapproval. We may draw their attention to a straight-forward question, and politely request a plain answer. (It is unlikely that it will be forthcoming.) If non-material things exist, what are they? How are they to be described? Significantly, there appears to be no positive word available. "Spiritual" suggests itself, but is unsatisfactory, because it would imply that those who disclaim materialism are all spiritualists. In fact, of course, materialism is a philosophy that involves the belief that only material things exist. Opponents of this view generate much confusion, not only by relating it to conduct, to which it has no connection, but by regarding abstractions and activities as things. Thoughts are activities of the brain, not entities. Love is an attitude of people who love. And is not energy (*pace* some atomic physicists) a function of matter?

Liberation of thought is, indeed, basic to happiness. We hear it asserted by Christians that it is natural for man to worship, but humanists point out that it is still more natural for man to think. Happiness depends intrinsically on the opportunity to think freely and to know that we are honest in our thought. Can we honestly look around us and believe in the reality of "another world", when only this world presents itself before us? The mental strain involved in the attempt has a needlessly painful and disturbing effect upon us. Released from the pursuit of an imaginary world, we can devote ourselves cheerfully to our experiences of the real one. Our thoughts are no longer clouded by vague and elusive gropings, nor cramped by the demands of religious faith. We can experience an intellectual enlightenment similar to that enjoyed by the scholars of the Renaissance, when they encountered the revival of classical learning and the excitement of experiment and discovery.

We would not, of course, suggest that happiness can be perfected in thought, regardless of whether or not we are free to acquire food, shelter and emotional satisfaction, all of which are essential to an entirely happy life. For, although the seeking of happiness should be man's chief concern, we recognise, as we said earlier, that complete happiness is unlikely to be possible; but, whereas we may be deprived of the means to act as we would wish, no one can rob us of mental satisfaction. This could, though, be an exceedingly pernicious doctrine, and we find it so in the hands of some religious people, who maintain that, provided mental happiness is secured – they may call it spiritual – physical or material happiness is unimportant, as the blessings of a future life will compensate us.

Incidentally, we meet here again the presumed distinction between physical or material on the one hand, and mental (possibly spiritual) on the other. So it would appear that non-material things may, perhaps, be mental, if not spiritual. We hope to explain a little later that this supposition is a false one.

Meanwhile, let us clearly appreciate the liberating and satisfying nature of our humanist position. A genuine sense of wonder at the mystery of existence is an emotional and scientific experience, not a religious one; for the latter is invariably mixed up with feelings of fear and guilt. If we believe that nature is in some way alive, or that there is a supernatural active agent in the universe akin to ourselves, but supposedly vastly superior to us, and to whom we are ultimately responsible, (This is the essence of the religious outlook), no objective attitude is possible. And all science is based on the assumption that nature is objective and predictable. This is the common expectation of human life. Those who want to include a world of supernatural events open up a bottomless pit of doubt and apprehension, for which there is no conclusive evidence whatsoever. It contradicts our ordinary experience – the plain testimony of our senses – and so imposes a harrowing mental conflict. We owe our very civilisation to science, to what we have discovered about nature; but, unless we can shake ourselves free of the idea that objective nature is at the same time embodying a subjective force, working for or against us – ignorance fostered this notion in the past – our lives will be ruined by emotional disturbances.

Of all the distressing inroads that religion makes on human happiness, the most damaging may well be in times of bereavement. Those who believe that the dead are "with them in spirit" are deprived of all comfort except that conveyed by fellow believers, most of whom are commonly too embarrassed to say very much, and no one else wants to hurt the feelings of those in distress by exposing the make-believe on which they rely. As we travel through life with our friends of a religious persuasion, only the view from the carriage window can be discussed – not a word about the nature of the journey. So when the end comes there is little preparation to deal with it. Those who have been brought up to trust in religion have only their spiritual mentors for comfort, and these they have largely ignored in the past and received no sustenance to help them face up to the normal impact of life, let alone its tragedies. So when the hungry sheep look up, they are not fed. Humanism offers plain acceptable nourishment, of which the main ingredient is a gratifying sense of mental serenity, for no unseen forces lurk in the shadows to disturb the feast.

Plain nourishment, yes. We need no "spiritual" trimmings to flavour the banquet that life lays out; but we should realise that our senses can provide untold fascination that far surpasses this metaphor. Do we really appreciate the variety, charm and richness of the world around us: the sound of music, the scents in our flower gardens, let alone all the beauty of nature and human art? Consider the sense of sight. Few will deny that it is the most rewarding of all the five. Trite and obvious perhaps – but if you doubt its supreme worth, close your eyes; or, better still, listen to those who, born blind, have an operation enabling them to see.

Cynics may remind us that we have bad as well as good sensations. They portray all the horrors and disasters that afflict the world. True, of course, but as humanists we are better able to cope with sadness than religious people who cling to the spurious consolations of an imaginary spiritual comforter. Moreover, our species is unique in evolutionary development in that kindness and care for others have emerged, and precariously seek a firmer foothold that will help us to climb to a higher expression of civilised values. There is little altruism in the rest of nature, but we can develop it and find pleasure in so doing. Thus, deprived members of our society will enjoy maximum satisfaction.

More cynics will argue that if we help the weak to breed, the physical quality of humanity will decline. Indeed, if civilisation is to have a future, human intelligence, which has so effectively produced our technology, will have to assert itself and achieve a rational plan for population control.

Meanwhile let us open wide our windows on the world. Let us not take leave of our senses!

"A poor life this, if, full of care,
We have no time to stand and stare."

FIVE

WHY THEN, DOES RELIGION STILL SURVIVE?

Misinterpreting one's actual experience.

When Saint Augustine wrote: "Thou hast made us for Thyself, O Lord, and our hearts will know no rest until they rest in Thee", the climate of the times led religious thinkers to assume that man had an emotional need for God. But we should be as easily persuaded otherwise. For if we look closely into our needs in a secular environment, we shall find that it is true to say that we depend upon each other. We seek the affection and approval of other people, and are miserable if estranged from them. We are happiest when involved in emotional, social or cultural activities: this is the attitude of the average person. There are exceptional people who appear to be self-sufficient, but even they will mostly try to justify their way of life in the eyes of the rest of us. A few seem to have a genuine inclination for religious rites and ceremonies, and we must try to be fair to those devout, ordinary people, for whom religion is a real and valued part of their lives. But most of us enjoy secular activities, which do not need forcing and carefully cultivating on Sundays.

Apart from fundamentalists, we see little spontaneous enthusiasm for religion. Even the conventional grace before meals is not often encountered, and it is not obvious that many people who would claim to be Christians do actually pray. Yet some form of prayer or meditation is an indispensable element in almost every type of religion, and in Christianity, the familiar form to most of us, is a basic commitment. Indeed, the psychological effect that can be derived from prayer should not be lightly dismissed, but it seems that only the weight of tradition and emotional involvement enable people to disregard the otherwise inescapable fact of its unreality. Communication with God can be such a painfully one-sided procedure, that it is seldom attempted in everyday life.

Let us, then, look more carefully at this rather puzzling situation. On the one hand ordinary people find little use for religion. (If questioned, many would vaguely support it, but it plays no leading role in their lives.) On the other we see that much that goes on in our society is geared to a religious tradition. Further, the impact of past enthusiasm is still very much with us. Vast cathedrals, for example, bear vivid testimony to one-time (and present) devotion. Visitors to these imposing buildings can be overwhelmed by the skill and dedication of the architects who designed them, the craftsmen who built them and the artists who adorned them. This is all very sad to humanists, who realise that magnificence, splendour or antiquity do not denote with certainty true doctrines. The religion that produced the pyramids and lasted longer than Christianity has so far survived, is now of interest only to scholars. But clearly we must not be tempted to stress popular indifference to religion, urging the conversion of churches into libraries or museums, without paying attention to the continued prevalence of religious belief in many quarters. Humanism must justify its claim that religion no longer satisfies the needs it did in the past. If we question the validity of what religious people call a spiritual view of life, we need not only to show that human experience can be more adequately interpreted in terms of a materialist one, but also to explain more plainly than we have so far, why religion, though lapsed from almost complete ascendancy, continues to exert so much influence. We have already discussed the emotional factor. We now examine some further incentives.

From the complex web of the history of religion we can extract one simple, but vital thread. Our ancestors found therein not only an inspiration for the conduct of their lives, but also an explanation of the existence of the universe. It seemed reasonable to regard God as its author. The processes of nature were little understood, so it was not difficult to believe that God was at work. The rainbow was his mercy-sign and calamities were an indication of his wrath. The potent and unexplained forces of nature suggested an almighty "spiritual" force, and this view prevailed until the discoveries of science gradually revealed many of the mechanisms of nature, and, what is of much greater importance, led to more critical thought. It became obvious to many that if God were to be postulated as the maker of the universe, a further question would arise: "Who made God?" The mystery is merely pushed one stage further back. It is not that we demand an explanation for everything, as our critics would like to maintain, telling us that it is still true that there are more things in heaven and earth than are dreamt of in our sceptical philosophy. What we object to are spurious explanations. Our experience is subjective and our understanding of nature is bound to be only partial, but we are not helped by answers which merely raise further questions.

Even among those who have abandoned the conception of God as the explanation of existence, few have freed their thinking from attachment to ways of expressing religious ideas that are a hangover from the days of unquestioning faith and times when "the gods" were regarded very objectively. As we have seen, language can be misleading, because words do not have to relate to objects which exist, in order to appear to make sense. "There are fairies at the bottom of the garden," for example, is a perfectly good sentence. In talking of religious matters we use the only language we have: that of everyday experience; and because the words have an intelligible meaning in their usual context, we are tempted to suppose that they have meaning when applied in a religious sense. If we were to hear that a person "survived" an accident, we would be in no doubt about the meaning; but when we are told that people "survive" death, we have no such understanding. It used to be argued that, as a watch implies a watch-maker, so the fact of the universe establishes the existence of a god who made it. We still occasionally meet this view, so it is worth pointing out that the word "made" loses its acceptable meaning when transferred from the activities of a watch-maker to those of God. Watch-makers use materials which they do not make. Whence came the materials available to God? Sentences such as "God 'speaks' to us" and "God 'loves' us" lack any straightforward meaning, unless God is envisaged as possessing human faculties. In fact, such words can be accepted only by suspending all critical judgement. It is their familiarity that helps them to survive. Sentences such as "We 'speak' to each other" and "We 'love' each other", can be so readily understood that it is taken for granted that the words have meaning when used in the religious context. Believers will concede that their meaning is not the same, but refuse to admit that they are inapplicable.

Of course, many philosophers have exposed the danger of the irresponsible use of words, but generally over the heads of ordinary people. Humanism draws attention to the palpable nature of the situation and asks whether it is honest to go on using words, once we realise their inadequacy.

At this point let us consider a word that tends to frighten people off humanism. If we do not believe in God or in any God-substitute, it is undeniable that we are atheists. But many seem to shudder at this drastic word, and use "agnostic", preferring to be on the safe side. For after all, they claim, who can prove that there is no God? However, the weakness of this attitude is that for practical purposes we are forced to decide. There are cases where this causes no hesitation. Consider fairies. Do agnostics suspend disbelief in them? But surely spirits and fairies are of similar essence. In the past this was frequently assumed. Shakespeare did not appear to recognise any difference. In *A Midsummer Night's Dream* the terms seem interchangeable. Puck is equally happy to be described as either. At the end of the play he actually invents a word which signifies both, hoping that "we shadows" have not offended the dreamers.

So as humanists we act as though there were no God. Otherwise we should not be humanists. But this does not imply that we adhere to a fixed dogmatism. Belief in atheism is as provisional as any other scientific belief. To live we need to make decisions and act upon them, and this scientists commonly do, taking into account the evidence available. We cannot know with absolute certainty what will happen tomorrow, but we do not hesitate to make preparation for what we expect to happen. Agnosticism is a concession to religious belief, because in leaving the option open, it implies that belief and disbelief have equal claim on us; whereas a humanistic experience of life makes it very plain that "God" is for all practical purposes an illusion.

Have we now included all that accounts for the survival of religion? No, of course there are other relevant factors, and one of them, the implication for morality, we shall deal with in the next chapter.

We should, perhaps, pause here to underline a fundamental consideration. Theologians get away with the most outrageous assertions because so many people fail to engage in serious thought. It is comfortable to allow the professional exponents of religion to go unchallenged because of the painful effects of the controversy – the intellectual and emotional disturbances we have already mentioned. This disinclination to think critically is understandable, for some arguments are complex; but we would again remind our readers that people should not be deterred, as it is the simple issues that are the important ones, and we address ourselves only to these.

The removal of restrictions on thought is a recurring theme in this book. Our discursive approach may continually lead us along well-trodden paths, but this should be helpful, for the country as a whole is unfamiliar. Many people have scarcely even heard of humanism, and we seek to open their eyes to a liberating and satisfying outlook.

SIX

MORALITY AT RISK?

We do not need supernatural support to lead a good life.

"Blessed are the pure in heart, . . ." Presumably the pure in heart are the well intentioned people, who, to the limit of their ability, lead blameless and praiseworthy lives. So let us consider how we identify them. What are their characteristics? They are friendly, kind, understanding and patient, so that it is difficult to upset them, and an atmosphere of relaxation and confidence surrounds them. They are unselfish and thoughtful concerning the needs of others. Honesty and sincerity ensure that they can be relied upon to fulfil their responsibilities. Offended only by oppression, injustice or prejudice, they will tirelessly support those who need their help.

Such, in varying degrees, are the qualities we look for in people we regard as good citizens and worthy members of society. But let us observe that in listing their desirable attributes we have made no mention of religion or religious beliefs. Do all these people go to church or practise some other form of religious activity? Obviously this is not the case, and the point we wish to stress is that there is no necessary connection between good conduct and religion. Many preachers foster the idea that non-belief is sinful. It probably is, but let us realise that sin, like the "problem" of suffering, is an invention of religious people. It is an offence against God, not necessarily against man. For if we wish to enquire about goodness, we consider deeds that are helpful to man. God need not enter the picture.

It seems most improper to confuse sin with anti-social behaviour. When we are reproached from the pulpit, urged to reform our conduct and given an account of the "good Christian life," this confusion is heaped upon us. Indeed it is widely prevalent: many people who find Christian theology unacceptable, claim nevertheless to be Christians because they do their best to follow the appropriate way of living. Thieving, drunkenness, hooliganism and the like are clearly bad for society, but to regard them as sins, that is, transgressions against divine law, is misleading. Secular law – the law that protects society – takes no account of sin. Provided we cause no disturbance and do not harm our neighbours, we can sin as much as we like. The criterion of an offence is the extent of its harm to society.

Can we then say that belief in God need not be an essential part of Christianity? Can one qualify by following Christ's way of life, without the need for any other question being asked? Unfortunately, a little consideration will reveal why few religious people would find this satisfactory. The dismissal of the traditional concept of God, although it may not alter the world in which popes, bishops and the clerical establishment can conduct their business, puts us well on the road to humanism. For if human welfare is the only relevant factor in defining the good life, clearly morality is not ruled out in the absence of religion.

We should keep these considerations before us when we meet the complaint that morals would collapse without the support of religion; realising also, of course, that any of the alleged benefits of religion have no bearing on the truth of its doctrines. But there are two further aspects of the case on which we should reflect. Firstly, it is doubtless true that supernatural beliefs have greatly helped to control human passions in the past, and, because of the confusion we have outlined, continue to play their part, though in a diminished role, as a steadying social influence. This means that humanists should recognise the need to establish morality on firmer ground; and here we are led to the second point: we must ask where, if not from religion, we can find the emotional inspiration that will assist us in defeating our selfish impulses, so that we can live together harmoniously.

Early social life was organised very largely on a religious basis, priests being the guardians of tribal or village prosperity. But as a more complex society developed, we see religion withdrawn into the background, and public affairs conducted on more secular lines. No uniform pattern can be defined, but an urbane and educated section of the community would come to find the gods dispensable. Educated Romans, for example, were well aware of the crudity of popular religious practices, as is indicated by the well known words of Cicero, wondering how the augurs could refrain from winking at each other when they passed in the streets. Religion was far from officially disregarded, but Roman law took charge of the citizens' welfare, and, incidentally, handed on institutions of great value to later civilisations. And in our own day, although clerical influence is still strong, especially in rural life and in the more archaic aspects of government, the church is no longer involved in the essential processes of civil administration.

The situation is well parodied in Samuel Butler's *Erewhon*. Visitors to this curious society found the people emotionally tied to their "Musical Banks". These issued coins which were very highly regarded, but had no purchasing power whatsoever, and everyone took good care that their purses were well lined with ordinary currency which would secure for them the normal necessities of life. Nor was it easy to obtain from the Erewhonians a clear description of the Bank's functions. They considered it proper to display some of its coins in their possession, but they were strangely reticent about the matter, and unwilling to reveal what it actually meant to them. Many of the Bank's buildings were ancient, venerable and extravagantly ornate. Business was accompanied by strange music emanating from dim recesses in the richly furnished interior, but the customers, never in any great numbers, and mostly elderly, seemed to creep in and out rather furtively; and its officials, though very well meaning and amiable people, tended to dress up as a separate class, and the more thoughtful of them did not give the impression of happiness in their jobs. How could they when so many of their fellow citizens paid but slight regard to the most precious of all institutions?

No, the world of make-believe, is an insecure foundation for any system of morality, for it can exercise no reliable influence on people's lives; and if offensive behaviour is on the increase, the fault does not lie in the neglect of religion. On the contrary, it may well be that good conduct should not have become associated with beliefs that cannot withstand the scrutiny of many thoughtful people.

Whence, then, do normal "decent" people derive their moral impulses? Some claim that we are living on the capital invested over a long period dominated by Christian ideals, and that we have Christianity to thank for our sense of right and wrong. But, as we have observed, although there may be some truth in this, we cannot rely on a system that has such fatal defects. The real key to the situation lies rather in the fact that we have certain social urges as well as selfish ones. Like other social animals, we instinctively behave as members of a group.

We shall refer to this again later, but, generally speaking, we can detect in ourselves two main sets of instinctive impulses: anti-social and social. The former are the more primitive and naturally possess us when we are young. Small children think the world is made for them and howl if they cannot get their own way. But we soon begin to learn that other people have a claim on our consideration. This realisation is part of the process of growing up and the basic aim of education, but we do not all achieve it with the same success. Some individuals remain two years old all their lives, expecting everybody to serve their interests. Society, however, exerts powerful pressures upon us to which we normally respond, because it is in our nature to do so. What we call our conscience – that system of thought instilled into us by our upbringing – helps to keep us on or near the straight and narrow path. Were this not the case, society would break up, and, as history shows, this has frequently happened. Successful communities are those which most effectively control man's primitive selfish instincts. This is done by removing our fears and giving us security. Social organisation should provide surroundings in which we can live in safety, and most of us, to a greater or lesser extent, respond by good behaviour. We repeat a simple fact: we are happiest when in tune with those around us. Blessed are the pure in heart (those who have adapted themselves to social demands), for they shall live contented lives – other things being equal, that is to say, provided their social needs are supplied.

Thus morality stems from the very structure of the society to which we belong, and any improvement we can bring about will be more effective than relying on outworn mythologies. True, political philosophers have said this before: make the people happy and they will be good, and our religious critics claim that this has always failed. "Man shall not live by bread alone." But what we need to realise is that the situation involves a struggle and presents a challenge. We cannot expect society to attain perfection while we stand and wait. It is a process of development, and successful living together makes many demands upon us. And let us not forget that attempts to serve up a diet other than bread – so-called spiritual nourishment – can hardly claim much success. But there is justification for hope. If we look back and trace the course of evolution from amoeba to man, or even from caveman to modern man, it is difficult to deny that progress has taken place in the past. So why should it not continue, remembering, of course, that such a survey covers mankind as a whole, not the fortunes of any particular civilisation?

Perhaps we should pause at this point to consider the views of those who do question the concept of progress when applied to the development of human morality. Are we really better disposed towards each other than cavemen? Has not our technological achievement resulted in the 20th century witnessing the worst yet so far as human behaviour is concerned? It certainly seems clear that, whereas man's technological ability has made great strides, his emotional control has not kept pace with it.

But hope may lie in the fact that man now has the means to assess his situation more accurately and come to realise that the good life is potentially within reach. Technical expertise has increased our efficiency in producing things that benefit us, such as better living conditions, as well as things that harm us, such as lethal armaments and the destruction of the environment. It is the latter that have intensified anxiety and fear.

Religion has lost its credibility and so can no longer cope with our needs. Humanism can, and the future depends on humanism. To survive we must co-operate with each other, and it does not seem unreasonable to hope that in time the dawn will break. Let us ask ourselves what sort of conduct makes us "feel good". Is it not that which brings us into pleasant relationships with other people? And are we so very different from the majority of our fellows in this respect?

Before we close a chapter in which we have claimed that religion is powerless to sustain morality, it is necessary to emphasise that it is also a positive danger to human progress. Religion fuels the fires of hostile encounters, especially when involved in group rivalries. Even entire nations pursue policies based on intolerant religious convictions.

We shall speak more of this in the next chapter.

SEVEN

CIVILISATION AT RISK?

Most religions claim to be peaceful, but they contain fundamentalist assumptions which encourage violence, disrupting free-thought and social stability.

In outlining some of the practical implications of humanist thought, we have not laid down any dogmatic assertions, but rather tried to encourage people to think. It is our hope, as expressed in Chapter 5, that a reasonable attitude will follow if we think honestly without emotional constraints, when facing up to the facts of our experience.

Continuing to further some understanding of humanism, let us turn again to its more theoretical aspects, but first assail a widespread belief that it is a kind of religion. Religious people would like to saddle us with the idea, because it enables them to support those humanist actions of which they approve, and further to claim that religion is a human necessity. But this cannot be allowed. If words are to have any meaning, we must associate religion with the supernatural. A religious person is "bound" (Latin: *religare*) to some alleged reality beyond nature, or, as philosophers would say, metaphysical. We may well echo St. Paul's words "If Christ is not risen, then is our faith vain", by our own admission that if there is any truth in the supernatural, humanism is utterly mistaken. The medieval monks used to write over the doors of their hostels "God encompasseth us". This appears to have been corrupted into the inn-sign "Goat and Compasses". For the monks, God and the supernatural were an ever-present and unquestioned reality. But we suggest that in the modern world it is widely accepted that Darwin and Freud have removed all grounds for restoring the supposed meaning of the caption. We shall refer to this view again later on in the chapter.

Meanwhile we will remind readers that religious people are

seldom disturbed by their blatantly improper use of language. We have given an example of this in Chapter 4, when we protested at the abuse of the word "material". Quite apart from their treatment of symbolic terms as though they were realities, (as when God is portrayed as loving and caring for us), they encourage the adoption of words which have no place in secular speech. Religion can easily slip in by a side door unless we insist that words such as "spiritual" have no practical meaning apart from a religious context. We recall a meeting of school governors at which the "spiritual" needs of the children were being discussed. When asked the meaning of the word, a member of the local authority replied "I suppose it means 'religious'." What is actually referred to, of course, are the needs which children have for emotional, intellectual, social and cultural fulfilment – all very much bound up with human relationships. To import "spiritual" values into a secular situation is indeed a damaging misuse of words, and humanists should not be tempted.

We turn now to the main theme of this chapter which is to show that humanism has prompted a new intellectual and emotional attitude since the Middle Ages, which has enhanced civilisation, whereas unrestrained religious influences have put it in danger.

But first let us point out that, generally speaking, although humanism was expounded by many Greek and Roman philosophers in classical times, and, having been nearly eclipsed during the Dark Ages, flourished again in the Renaissance, and on through the Enlightenment of the 17th and 18th centuries, it was not until modern times that its outlook became wholly secular and posed a serious threat to religion.

By way of illustrating this rather generalised approach we will briefly draw attention to Renaissance Humanism, and indicate how it differed from, but prepared the way for, the present philosophy which excludes the concept of God. To this end we cannot do better than look back to the popular series of television programmes broadcast in 1969 by the late Lord Clark, then Sir Kenneth Clark, entitled *Civilisation*. These attractively illustrated lectures were published by the B.B.C. and John Murray in 1969 and re-printed in paperback in 1971. They traced the course of civilisation, relating its progress to the standard of art (as the most revealing expression of human faculties) and asked in what it actually consisted, which forces advanced it and which brought it near to destruction. Civilisation barely survived in the Dark Ages, but revived towards the close of the Middle Ages as the Renaissance prompted in man a new attitude towards nature and himself. So we propose to discuss that part of Kenneth Clark's narrative which deals with Renaissance Humanism, as much of it concurs with the ideas that we are stressing in these pages.

Kenneth Clark told how in 1498 there arrived at Oxford an impoverished scholar who was to become the greatest internationalist of his day, the Dutchman, Erasmus. Kept on the move not only by his own mental restlessness, but also by the ever-threatening danger of the plague, he spent enough time in England to ensure this country a place in any survey of civilisation. He enriched the circle of Sir Thomas More, and by his intellectual charm became greatly admired all over Europe. Much of his influence resulted from correspondence. He wrote many letters to his many friends, for, typical of all humanists, he set a high value on friendship. (We repeat here our warning that we must beware of supposing that humanists have a monopoly of this civilising virtue).

Kenneth Clark went on to explain how the invention of printing enabled Erasmus to become the first journalist. Although he wrote in Latin, he was able to spread new ideas and stimulate more readers than had ever enjoyed such writings before. His In *Praise of Folly* attacked all areas of authority in his time: popes, kings, monks, scholars, war, theology – none was allowed to escape. Yet he took no forthright stand. He did not believe in protests that led to revolutionary splits, as did the religious enthusiast, Luther, who unleashed so many elements of destruction a few years later: both sides in the religious controversy proclaiming themselves instruments of God's wrath. And what struck Kenneth Clark as extraordinary was the huge following that nevertheless supported Erasmus, showing that many people, even in times of upheaval, really yearn for tolerance, reason and simplicity of life – in fact, for civilisation.

Let us also note Kenneth Clark's brief reference to Montaigne and Shakespeare. The former he regarded as the greatest humanist of the mid-16th century. He was well aware of the antagonisms provoked by the Reformation, reflecting that in trying to make themselves angels, men transform themselves into beasts. He therefore largely avoided public life, becoming an intellectual recluse. (This was a figure new to European civilisation, although plentiful enough in eastern countries.) Such was the abhorrence of the wars of religion felt by the most civilised man of the century! Indeed, Montaigne qualified as a humanist in the modern sense (an opinion not expressed by Kenneth Clark), for he was completely sceptical about the Christian religion, being resolved to look at the other side of every question and accept the verdict of honest self-examination. He delighted in passing on his discoveries, and so "invented" the essay, which was to remain an accepted form of humanist communication for three centuries, from Francis Bacon to Charles Lamb.

According to Kenneth Clark one country at the end of the 16th century, though brutal and disorderly, did afford opportunities for those with intellectual energy, without forcing them to retreat to an isolated tower. This was Elizabethan England – the background of Shakespeare. He regarded the mature Shakespearean plays as the poetic fulfilment of Montaigne's intellectual honesty, but embodying a far more uncomfortable scepticism. He thought that in Shakespeare, Montaigne's detachment was replaced by passionate engagement: instead of the essay, there was the urgent communication of the stage. Further, he suggested that Shakespeare must be the first, and probably the last, supremely great poet to have been without religious belief. Before the Reformation broke up Christendom, such lines as these would have been unthinkable:

> "Life..............is a tale
> Told by an idiot, full of sound and fury,
> Signifying nothing."

Kenneth Clark was himself saddened by the tragic split which for him left an emptiness difficult to be faced. For humanists, of course, there is the satisfaction of the positive side of secular thinking; but, nevertheless, we find his discourse extremely stimulating, reminding us that the Renaissance, based on the enthusiastic scrutiny of the pagan world of Greece and Rome, changed man's outlook completely, leading to the view that the proper study of mankind is man, and enabling the pursuit of science to become progressively more scientific.

We wrote to Kenneth Clark at the time of his lectures, expressing admiration of them and enclosing an early draft of this chapter. He replied saying that he was not an out and out humanist in the sense of disbelieving entirely in the supernatural, but he thought it right that such a case should be stated and expressed his approval of our attempt to do so.

As Kenneth Clark admitted, generalisations are unavoidable when discussing the movements of human thought. However some can, perhaps, be allowed if any significant conclusions emerge. We ask readers to keep this in view, as it seems appropriate here to try to sort out two contradictory strands of religious awareness. In so doing we must attempt to distinguish between deism and theism. Of course, *theos* was the Greek word for God, and *deus* the Roman word, but they have come to carry divergent connotations.

The humanists of the Renaissance re-discovered the works of man, but they were mostly deeply religious deists (defined in the O.E.D. as those who believe in God on the grounds of reason and not biblical revelation). Few had any doubts concerning the works of God. Later on, as we have noted, Newton regarded his discoveries as revealing divine achievements. This belief in a transcendent "deus" – the "God out there" – coexists for most religious people with an experience of the immanent "God within", viewed less as a creator than as a personal God – the "theos" who rules their lives.

Up to now we have not had much to say about theology, for the tenets of theologians are so obscure that people stand little chance of enlightenment, though theologians themselves seem not unduly worried. Most of them have survived quite well after swallowing such incredible doctrines as the Trinity and other mentally indigestible concepts. However, in Chapter 1 we contended that Darwin has disposed of the "God without" and we supplied evidence to support this view. We now suggest that it is equally obvious that Freud has been chiefly responsible for undermining the "God within". Here we enter the field of mental life, and we shall not depart from our aim of keeping psychology simple. We merely point out that he exposed the roots of religion in the need for a father-figure. The *O.E.D.* indicates that theism involves a belief in a personal God, and Freud convincingly demonstrated that craving for the tender care of a benevolent providence was a hangover from childhood desires.

Notwithstanding the disclosures of scientists, philosophers and psychologists, these two bewildering concepts of the divine existence persist. For believers God is both immanent within them and somehow transcendent everywhere else. We regard these two illusions as equally dangerous, and we fear that civilisation is not safe in the hands of those who ignore the evidence and continue to cultivate supernatural dispensations. Past inquisitions, massacres and witch-hunts and present sectarian and communal persecutions, not to mention the excesses of theocratic regimes, amply confirm these fears.

Any historical survey prompts us to reflect uneasily that there is a delicate balance on which our survival depends. Those who believe that God helps them to make history and that their lives must be ordered to express his will, can be ruthless in their determination to obey him. But humanists realise that civilisation depends entirely on human effort and co-operation. Social life presents a demanding challenge and some cannot stand up to it. But those who complain of the strains and stresses which individuals suffer at the hands of society, seldom reflect on the incalculable benefits which social organisation confers upon us. Admittedly there are emotional tensions within ourselves, for our animal instincts have yet to be completely reconciled to urban life. Living together in cities is a comparatively recent development, a vast period of tribal existence having preceded it. Nevertheless, we would do well to see to it that civilisation has come to stay. Chaos resulting from its breakdown would benefit no one, least of all those most distressed by social pressures.

How easily we take civilisation for granted. If cast away on a desert island, we would avoid the frustrations and anxieties which are liable to weigh so heavily on individuals, as masses of their fellows surge around them; but most of us would soon yearn for the advantages of civilised life, now beyond our reach. We could not assume that such assets as the Bible and Shakespeare would be shipwrecked with us.

Incidentally, lest some may wonder that we include the Bible among the fruits of civilisation, let us end this chapter with a reminder that a secular attitude provides a wider field for emotional and intellectual enjoyment than a religious one. Those who regard the Bible as inspired by God, cannot absorb it as poetry. The superb verses: "Remember now thy Creator in the days of thy youth. . . ." can be fully appreciated only by those who have no religious commitment to disturb the emotional impact.

Let us allow the enlightenment of science and psychology, which was far less available to the humanists of the Renaissance, to reveal the value of a secular humanist enthusiasm. We shall find that those deep-seated human needs, which were formerly and still are so widely satisfied by religion, can be more peacefully and rewardingly met by human understanding and friendship.

EIGHT

LIVING TOGETHER

Divinely inspired dogma imperils friendship.

So far we have made no attempt to deal with any aspect of humanism exhaustively. We have discussed themes and suggested attitudes, hoping to show that a learned outlook is not necessary to understand it. All we need is clear thinking and a firm control over our emotions, so that we can interpret our modern experience in terms that do not contradict it, instead of clinging to explanations derived from the mythology of a by-gone view of life.

We have raised matters that are largely theoretical, dealing with the way we think, rather than the way in which we act. But we have not forgotten that life is for living. Confined to an ivory tower and immersed in thought, we shall not find much satisfaction for ourselves nor give any to others. So to what sort of action does humanist thinking direct us? Were psychologists to explore its implications, would they point to any specific propensities or inclinations? We want now to ask whether there are any distinctive practical implications that result from humanist ideas.

Giving up religious belief is often criticised as being purely negative; but on the contrary it leads to the most positive situation it is possible to meet. What is so fruitless and frustrating is trying to establish relationships between ourselves and God. True, people living their ordinary lives, pay little attention to the problem and find religion most of the time totally irrelevant to them; but few can escape the impact of its pressure especially on radio and television, and all can well be reminded that when we turn our attention away from spiritual affiliations and towards contact with each other, we encounter demanding, but if successful, very rewarding and emotionally fulfilling experiences.

41

We may begin by understanding that humanism, unlike religion, offers the prospect of uniting mankind. A glance at the world situation will reveal the fractious nature of policies influenced by religion. The sub-continent of India was partitioned on religious grounds, and we do not have to look beyond Ireland and the Middle East for other examples of social conflict closely bound up with religion.

One of the purposes of this book is to expose these harmful effects, but without in any way suggesting that humanists are more eager to promote friendship and peace than religious people. We do not, like many Christians, announce a superior ethical approach to life. So often we hear the statement "It is our Christian duty", when some personally distasteful, but socially helpful attitude is called for. The implication is, of course, that generous actions are to be expected of Christians, and less likely to be practised by unbelievers.

It is worth pausing to stress that we should not announce a humanist ethic that informs people how they ought to conduct their lives. If we do this we enter the field of politics, for the improvement of human society is basically a political matter. Rises in living standards have been achieved by Acts of Parliament, but humanism provides no clear directive indicating which political party we should join. A similar confusion arises about supporting organisations working for peace.

We need to ask the question "Whence comes the best motivation?" Religion certainly inspires many people to sacrifice their lives to the care of others, but, being based on an illusion, it is dangerously misleading, and can prompt irrational means that defeat worthy ends. Humanism provides a far more reliable motivation. The absence of a supernatural agency leaves us no option but to support each other, and there is an instinctive drive in our nature (of which we shall say more later) that inclines us to avoid anti-social behaviour. But just how we should respond to this is an individual decision. By all means let us advocate the way we think best and join with those we regard as most able to achieve both justice and liberty. This we should do as members of society and not claim that there is a humanist programme superior to that of religious people. It is a human or humanitarian attitude that we need, and this can be expected of all human beings. All can join in, but humanism supplies a motive that is less likely to lead us astray. This will become clearer if we discuss the matter further.

It is, of course, widely recognised that owing to the efficiency of modern communications and the pressing problems which face mankind as a whole, nationalism is out of date. But the various religions, each having developed along with the races or communities to which they belong, have become imbued with national traditions and sentiments, and so are incapable of motivating international harmony. True, religious people hotly deny this, and claim to be devoted to the ideal of the brotherhood of man. But they are deceiving themselves. Religions are so firmly attached to national or racial groupings that any attempt to unify people on a religious basis is sure to fail. We can imagine the futility of suggesting to Arabs or Jews that they should sink their religious differences. Divinely revealed truth demands unquestioning obedience, and the prescribed practices are usually, as we have said, deeply imprinted on national cultures.

But humanism knows nothing of national boundaries. It places no obstacle in the way of world government, population control, conservation of the world's resources and their development for all mankind. This book happens to be written in English and assumes a particular national background, and, incidentally, we may regard ourselves as fortunate to live in a relatively open society, where a book on humanism, if not widely acceptable, is at least likely to appear. Our national situation, however, need not blind us to our membership of the human race. The concept of world citizenship should never be far from our thoughts. We have an inspirational motive here far superior to anything religion can provide.

We cannot over-stress the fact that religious people are no less friendly than humanists. It is their faith that is divisive. Let us recall our thoughts about hope, for hope, not faith, can unite us and is such a satisfying feature of humanism. Faith makes no demands other than unquestioning belief. The outcome is entirely in the hands of divine providence. But hope is practical. Unlike faith, it is concerned with things that can actually occur, for which we can plan and by our own efforts help to bring about. It is rational to embrace an attitude of hope, for human beings have the necessary resources if only they will allow friendship to prevail. That we are unlikely to see the fulfilment of this hope ourselves need not depress us. We do not expect it, for, as we have pointed out, many the world over are acting in the denial of friendship and goodwill. But meanwhile in our thought and action we can become citizens of the world depicted in our vision.

We have suggested that we cannot lay down specific humanist rules or even guide-lines, and yet to the question "What should humanists do?" there is an unequivocal answer. It goes without saying that we should do the same things as all other people of good will: strive to help the weak, comfort the distressed and join with those we think most able to cure human ills. But in so doing we are expressing our social instincts and these are just as likely to be manifested in religious people.

Most of us may feel that we are very small fish swimming in a very large pond, but, to pursue the metaphor, when we see so many of our fellow swimmers hooked up to fallacious lines of thought, our priority is to unhook them. In other words, the promotion of humanism may be the first requirement. But humanism has no monopoly of good intentions, and working together may solve many of the problems of living together. Where areas of difference arise, as in the choice of political affiliations, we can express our support for the preservation and extension of democratic institutions. It is not presumptuous to claim that democracy is the child of humanism, for it is plainly at risk where dogmatic religious motivations prevail. Many religious people are, of course, staunch democrats, but their real inspiration stems from those kindly human dispositions which we all share. It is these that promote tolerance, understanding and successful living together.

Alone among the animals with whom we share Planet Earth we have developed a degree of self-consciousness that enables us to have some knowledge of what we are doing. Thus we have the potential means of taking control of our own future, and yet with our human technology we have devised methods of mutual destruction unsurpassed by any other species. We see many elaborate devices by which some animals trap and eat each other. Certain colonies of ants invade and enslave other colonies, but the credit for maximum horror must go to humanity.

Sadly, living together presents us with problems that have so far been intractable. All through our evolutionary past our relationships with each other have been critical. But now a new challenge arises. As post-Darwinians, we have a better understanding of our nature, and this may lead to a realisation that mutual co-operation is our vital concern. A reminder that we are all human beings may seem trivial, but its implication is important. We are products of the biological process of that mysterious system known as nature. We have no supernatural affiliations. Perhaps the most outrageous "con" ever perpetrated or self-inflicted on the human race is the notion that we share the earth with a spirit world. We have discussed how this dualistic illusion may have originated, but it is time now that we came of age and recognised the manifest deception. It took a child to expose the pretence of the emperor's new clothes. Perhaps thinking people will at last protest at the nakedness of spirits decked out only in the imagination of their sponsors. Seeking a spiritual reality will inevitably divert us from the real world of human endeavour. Surely our imaginative insight is not so bankrupt that we cannot relate it to the evidence of our senses, without the need to fall back on to myths and wishful thinking.

NINE

HAS LIFE ANY PURPOSE?

A cosmological purpose is an anthropomorphic fallacy.

Humanism is sometimes criticised because it does not give meaning to life as religion claims to do. It seems to have no answer to the question: "What are we here for?" Can humanists show that there is any purpose in existence?

In reply let us first consider the anthropomorphic implication of this question. It assumes the biblical myth that there is someone out there – a personal "God" – who has planned the whole project and executed a grand design. But, as we have previously pointed out, if we look around us and examine our experience carefully, we shall find that we inhabit one world: a place where other people, other living things and inanimate objects comprise the totality of the objects of our awareness. The effects which are generally interpreted by religious people as evidence of another world arise from the richness and variety of our mental life, the power of our imagination and our relationships with other people. This material (or, as scientists more commonly term it, physical) world of sense experience does not imply the existence of a non-physical world, which as its exponents so confidently assure us, is just as real, but cannot be explored by scientists.

Dismissing this purposeful instigator certainly leaves us with a mystery which defies understanding, but nothing is gained by supposing that there are even more mysterious supernatural forces in our environment. We can be so easily confused and misled by the clever debating points advanced by the professional clerical establishment: people who are mostly sincere and wholly dedicated to human welfare. They have invested all their emotional capital in the faith in which they were nurtured or to which they have been converted. "To the Greeks, foolishness . . .", but these confessors are not fools. Indeed, many are thoughtful people and highly qualified academically. We must not dismiss them out of hand, but we have to face up to a tragedy. Many religious believers are so friendly and filled by benevolent feelings, that they cannot bring themselves to contemplate a universe that is unfeeling. For them it is unthinkable that we should not be in the hands of a purposeful, kindly providence. But benign behaviour is found only in living organisms – an attribute of our own species, if we will but cultivate it. We cannot impart our passions to the inanimate world. No personification of nature will accord it concern for us or remove its mystery.

People need to clarify and simplify their thoughts. This we can afford to do, for there is no need to become involved in the complexities of space-time, relativity and other notions understood by physicists. On a basis of simple thought we postulate infinity in all directions. We cannot comprehend it, but it seems a necessary concept. Should some limit or boundary be set, we have to ask what is beyond it. Clearly it makes rubbish of any local specifications – some unique dispensation governing the fate of one minute drop in the cosmic ocean. And how can "world without end" be an honest expression? We know perfectly well that the world will end, as the sun goes into decline like other stars.

How did the universe originate? To be told that there was a "big bang" explains little. It may appear a presumptuous suggestion, in view of the weighty scientific support for the theory, but surely there must have been some cause that detonated the explosion. What was this "singularity" that scientists want to invent as a one-off miracle? We seem to have abandoned Genesis only to come up with something hardly more credible. Nor does mystification lead us anywhere. "In the beginning was the word" begs all imaginable questions. Infinity of time and space utterly confounds our understanding, but it must invalidate any religion which claims to reveal final truth, as Christianity does. We contemplate the universe and we meet mystery, but there is no reason for introducing mysticism. Indeed, it is significant that the considerable volume of science fiction which has accompanied our modern space consciousness, does not appear to have suggested that there is more than one world for extra-terrestrial beings. Monsters and alien personalities have many lurid qualities and strange powers, but we hear very little of their religion; nor do their destinies seem to be controlled by a supernatural power, as is alleged of earth people. Of course, religious themes or backgrounds are seldom met with in earth-bound fiction – another indication of the secular nature of our interests.

As we noted in Chapter 3, it is sometimes claimed that science answers the question "How?" and religion the question "Why?". Can purpose be implied in the latter? Let us now examine the matter a little further. If we ask how a man caught a train, the answer describes the measures he took to leave home on time and reach the station before the train left. If we ask why he caught it, the answer provides some reason, such as his desire to undertake the journey. In this case the question "Why?" certainly involves purpose, but one devised by a human brain. If we ask why the volcano erupted or why the wind blew, the answers deal with the circumstances prevailing at the time, and the answer to the question "How?" reports the mechanism involved. Scientists are equally interested in both questions, which, in fact, are frequently the same when we enquire about natural phenomena.

So to the question "Is there any transcendental purpose in the universe?" we can confidently reply that there is none. For, as we have explained, there would need to be some conscious animate entity to entertain the purpose, and we have no knowledge of any. We are so imbued with this anthropomorphic fallacy that we fail to recognise its absurdity. To assume an "intelligence behind creation" without the necessary basis for it gives the word no meaning. Surely we have no experience of intelligence apart from its manifestation in a brain. Animal brains display it to varying degrees and human brains somewhat more so. We are speaking of a mental process, and it is really quite inconceivable that there should be a kind of floating intelligence somewhere independent of a brain. So purpose, being a function of thought, is most unlikely to be found anywhere in the universe unless it can be related to a thinker equipped with bodily organs.

However, purpose is present all the time. Our own purposes pervade our lives, and we would do well to concentrate on directing them to worthwhile ends, rather than harassing our brains to envisage some inscrutable destiny. An exceedingly satisfying aspect of humanism is the realisation that we have but one life to live. We need not waste our time and resources in anxious concern about an imaginary future life, and in so doing spoil our chances of making the most of the present one. Think of one of the many daunting problems we invent for ourselves. If the countless millions of our ancestors still exist as spirits, what does this mean, where are they, what are they doing, how do they communicate with each other and how do they avoid overcrowding? It may be claimed that spirits do not take up any room and other *ad hoc* arguments may be deployed, but such ludicrous speculations are unresolved. On the other hand, if we accept our mortality, we can achieve great satisfaction from co-operating with other people to improve what the world has to offer us. It is far better to accept the mystery that science discloses – indeed, to delight in it and share however slightly in the fascinating quest that is inseparable from its continuous unravelling – better this than to insult our intelligence by grasping at an unintelligible solution.

We need also to realise that the exponents of some celestial purpose actually undermine human morality. There is a traditional tendency in religious thought to leave all the initiative in the hands of God. We are too sinful to save ourselves. God must come to the rescue. But in reality we shall not meet with good behaviour in our world unless we put it there, take responsibility for it and teach it to our children. In this respect criticism of religion is a very positive thing. We make no claim to a superior moral purpose, as religious people frequently do, but urge that progress depends entirely on human effort.

As for the mystery of existence, perhaps we may compare our situation to waking up in a strange room and finding we have lost our memory. Such questions as "Where are we?" and "What are we doing here?" would immediately spring to our lips. However, being unaware of the answers, and being unable to examine anything beyond the room itself, we would have to confess our ignorance. We would be forced to conclude that explanations were, in the absence of reliable evidence, no more than guesses, and we would be irritated by those who kept insisting that certain unlikely stories could truly account for our circumstances. Interesting they might be, but no alleged revelation would make them plausible.

But in time our acquaintance with the room would reveal a treasure-house of wonder and delight, and we would find possible a fellow-feeling for one another, strong enough to calm our doubts and misgivings and prompt further exploration and discovery.

If our position is something like this, the fact that we cannot solve our problems or discover how they arose, need not diminish the zeal of our natural curiosity. It would be a pity for that to be repressed by the mistaken idea that some fundamental truth has been gratuitously provided. An objective and careful description of our surroundings, and an honest attempt to see things uninfluenced by national or cultural bias, refusing, that is, to accept any label other than that of human beings – such are the disciplines involved in the challenge of humanism: a challenge that our very nature urges us to accept. Man does not wish to live by bread alone.

TEN

APPROACHING THE QUESTION
"DO WE HAVE FREE CHOICE?"

*We try to think this one out, but does it
make any difference?*

By now readers may have realised that this is not a detailed and
methodical study of humanism, but an attempt to describe some
aspects which make it clear that people need not suffer from the
indigestible half-baked items appearing on the menus cooked up
by caterers of metaphysical meals.

We are aiming to show how humanism enables us to feel at
home in the world, removes the anxiety caused by the fear of
death and opens up the prospect of uninhibited enjoyment and
appreciation of people, places and things. But we should not
neglect to stress the necessity of an adequate standard of living.
We can so easily comprise a middle-class movement of those who
are free from impoverishment and largely unaffected by the
struggle that many have to endure to make ends meet. We
therefore recognise the need to achieve an open society in which
freedom and justice do not compete. We do this not necessarily as
humanists, for most religious people share the same concern, but
because we are aware that only human resources are available. No
divinity will lead the way. It is the responsibility of all of us to find
the best political and economic policies. We will expand these
ideas in a later chapter; suffice it to say now that good social
behaviour cannot be expected from those oppressed by poverty
and consequent ill health. Nor have deprived people much
opportunity to exercise the clarity of thought necessary to expose
the misleading arguments of the various purveyors of a mystical
approach to life.

Our emphasis on clear thinking has been mainly directed
towards plain and common sense issues. We have found from our

actual contact with people's ideas and behaviour that humanism satisfies both our reason and emotions; and it may be helpful to dwell on this briefly before giving some thought later in this chapter to coping in simple terms with a theoretical matter where philosophers commonly encounter heavy weather.

Our reason suggests that no final solution to the mystery of existence is possible and we are not emotionally content unless we make every effort to be honest in our thought. As we have said, it is very easy to assume the validity of familiar words which do not actually refer to anything real. We speak freely of truth, beauty and goodness, overlooking the fact that we do not experience these concepts. What we do experience are true statements, beautiful things and people who do good deeds. It is the people and things that are real, not the abstract concepts. Incidentally, people and things are material, and we should welcome any evidence that we are living in a materialistic world, for such a description is not a slur on our times, but an invitation to speak honestly, to cultivate and appreciate those beautiful things around us and to live in harmony with other people. There is nothing to gain if we seek some "spiritual" reality beyond our natural experience. We shall not find it. But we can think about it. And, because the world imposes little restriction on our thoughts, we should in all honesty ask ourselves just what it is we are thinking about. Not that we advocate the disuse of abstract terms, such as beauty and the like. Our point is that we should not infer from them the existence of some abstract reality.

We have drawn attention to the widespread influences which aim to condition us against the impact of materialism. Now before we become further immersed in the practical implications of humanist ideas, let us try in this chapter to consider another philosophical notion which is distasteful to some and puts them off our theme. We refer to the dislike of what professional philosophers call determinism. Are we really free to direct our thoughts consciously and honestly, or have we no choice in the matter? Is everything caught up in a continuous stream of cause and effect? This is sometimes said to follow from a scientific view of life, if no allowance is made for the influence of "spiritual" factors which are supposed to lie outside the area of knowledge covered by scientists.

Much philosophical brooding has not resolved the problem, but it can at least be expressed simply. If, as scientific enquiry needs to postulate, every event is caused by a previous event, we must regard all happenings as the necessary results of previous ones, that is, they are determined by what went before. In fact, a so-called event can be identified only for convenience, as a continuous flow is proceeding all the time.

This places us in a puzzling situation. On the one hand we act without question on the expectation that certain effects can be relied upon to follow certain causes. We would be very surprised if, when we dropped a stone, it did not fall to the ground, and we would look closely for some unsuspected cause that had prevented it. But on the other hand, what happens to the common assumption that we have free choice? A fixed chain of cause and effect seems to remove the possibility of our doing anything about it. And if we have no choice in the matter, how can we be blamed for anything we do? Christians base their whole concept of sin on man's ability to respond to God; and any system of morality would seem to collapse if we cannot choose between right and wrong because all our actions are the inevitable consequences of previous ones.

Certainly it is easy to state the problem, but less so to arrive at a solution. However, we can perhaps see some light if we decline to get caught up in the artificial fogs that tend to envelop the discussions of the experts. Not that we expect to be completely satisfied, but we may find the matter worth looking into.

We seem to be faced by three possible conclusions. The first asserts that freedom is an illusion. After all, we were not born free. We did not ask to be born, so at what stage did we acquire this capacity to rule our own lives? The second takes the opposite view. Nothing prevents us from acting freely in any given situation. The third, a compromise, suggests that our freedom is partial, being frequently limited by circumstances beyond our control.

Some degree of determinism seems obvious in the normal conduct of our lives. We take it for granted that certain results will follow specified actions, and if they do not, we merely suppose that we were unaware of the causes that actually operated. Thus we can forecast events with an accuracy "determined" by the extent of our knowledge of the relevant circumstances. This applies to people as well as things. If we know a person intimately, we can anticipate his reaction; of another we may not know sufficient to judge how he will act. Indeed, we frequently use the word when we just mean cause, as in the sentence: "Demand determines supply." Here we regard the amount of what is supplied as depending on, or caused by, the extent of the demand. And there seems to be no alternative to this view. If things are not determined, how else can we regard them? The causes that led to any given situation could not have been otherwise. If they had been, the situation in question would not have arisen.

Thus it may look as though we support contradictory ways of thinking without suffering any mental discomfort. For hand in hand with a belief in cause and effect, we have a general acceptance of what is called chance. On reflection, however, there is little conflict, because we can define chance as the absence of observable cause. So when we read "And by chance there came down a certain priest that way", we do not conclude that his journey was uncaused. No doubt he had a reason for it, although this did not help the robbers' victim, who had to wait for the equally "chance" arrival of the Samaritan.

Chance, then, may be reconciled with a deterministic view of things. Can we escape? The dictionary defines determinism as the theory that action is determined by causes independent of the will, and this reminds us that we are concerned with mental occurrences, and we may, perhaps, draw a distinction between the behaviour of the forces outside us and our response to them.

We do not regard the will as a faculty, but rather as the way we think when we are making a decision. Having a weak or strong will denotes our treatment of the decisions we have made. And here we meet what does appear to be a contradiction. For we do habitually assume that we are free to choose and that we can keep to our choices if we have sufficient will-power. But this, of course, is difficult to tie in with a deterministic view. Is there some special exemption that frees our thoughts from the determinism that applies to the things around us? What causes our thoughts? Like external events, they appear as a continuous flow, any given thought arising from previous ones. But these were our own thoughts, so perhaps we may regress to a limited freedom here. However, one thing is very clear: if our thinking is determined, we are quite unaware of it. We do not hesitate to assume responsibility. "I'm glad I did not do that." No suggestion arises that our choice was inevitable.

If, then, all or some of our experiences are determined, it is not a matter of practical significance. The important thing is that we feel free. Even the suspicion that it may be otherwise need not alarm us. After all, we have to accept the situation. Who would want to sit down helplessly and complain that activity is pointless because it is all fixed anyway? We can enjoy our brief swim in the stream of life without being displeased if the current carries us along. There are times, especially if we are absorbed in our experiences, when we feel quite free of it.

Further, it is not difficult to realise that the illusion, if such it is, has a key role to play in our lives. Without it we would be unable to attain that quality of existence that human consciousness makes possible. Civilisation demands a sense of moral responsibility, and our social training should in most cases have taken care of this. But decisions do not come out of the blue. If we decide to make an effort and to hold ourselves responsible for our own actions, and, perhaps, for some of the actions of others, that decision can be regarded as due to factors in the environment (which we currently experience) and in ourselves (built up by past experience). But the fact that the decision has a cause does not reduce its value to society, make it any less stimulating to us or imply that our own initiative was not responsible. Were we to swell the ranks of those who recognise no responsibility to their fellows, society would suffer even more acutely from disruptive outbursts. If we feel free and responsible, we can express that feeling in socially fruitful conduct. Nor is the area of illusion as extensive as it may appear: the feeling of freedom and the consequences of this feeling are real enough. We have a vivid and convincing experience of going through the process of choosing. That we may be deluded is an interesting theoretical supposition, but not a matter of vital concern – in marked contrast to the illusions of religion, which, like some uncalled-for off-stage effects, merely serve to confuse the drama of life.

We would remind readers who have been irritated by this discursive chapter that one of our main aims as humanists is to clarify our thoughts and simplify issues where possible, so that we may be more effective in dealing with the real challenge that faces humanity, namely, social conduct. We have yet to learn how best to live together, and conserve the resources that nature provides, instead of going to war about them.

Let us pursue this theme just a little longer. Although economic problems usurp most of our attention and appear to be at the bottom of our discontent, they are solvable. We should not personify nature as a parsimonious provider. Our anti-social instincts are the basic cause of human ills, and here religion plays an unfortunate role. It stimulates passions based on a misinterpretation of human nature and leads to insoluble conflicts. Revealed religion is no more than one group's picture of an imaginary divinity and clashes irreconcilably with that of others. Further, to a large extent it impairs human effort. It can even discourage such measures as birth-control, which really could ease our troubles, and, instead, urges less reliable solutions.

So an attempt to clarify our thoughts is no futile exercise. We do not need to grasp the details of intricate scientific systems, for, as we have tried to show, the important issues are simple and centre round our attitude to life. Are we free to take charge of our own evolution and what are the goals we should strive most urgently to achieve? Does anything prevent us from regarding friendship as the most valuable of all human assets?

Completely unhindered freedom may be unreal, and many the world over are disregarding friendship and goodwill, so we cannot expect to see a desirable society ourselves. But our hope is that one day it may come about, and meanwhile, by kind action and clear thinking, we may become its citizens without delay. We will be replacing religion by humanism.

ELEVEN

TOWARDS A HUMANIST PSYCHOLOGY

Removing the "psyche" from psychology.

This book is addressed to thoughtful people, but we have already stressed that humanism is most likely to find support with those who do not have to struggle to keep their heads above water in a society that threatens their security and is a source of emotional tension. Deprived people tend to cling to the safety of traditional beliefs. For, as we have said, our theme is a radical one. To cope with it we need to live in an open society where ideas are not constrained either by political or economic strait-jackets. In seeking to demonstrate that we live in one world – the world of material things – and in claiming that we can have no knowledge of any other reality, we undermine very cherished assumptions that exert a powerful influence in our society.

In this chapter we shall make some demands on people's thinking, calling not for advanced intellectual reasoning, but for an attempt to clarify certain ideas, while still keeping them simple. So again we point out that this is most likely to happen in an open and caring society. The satisfaction of getting one's thoughts sorted out and becoming an armchair philosopher is best achieved when supported by an adequate standard of living. We need to be able to afford the armchair. Economic, as well as intellectual freedom is necessary. But if people are free to think, we can expect a new approach. And new it is. Humanism liberates our thoughts. As we explore and interpret our experience of life, trying to be honest in the process and not allowing wishful thinking or emotional attachments to cloud our vision, we become aware that only through sense perception can we gain any information of the world around us. But this attitude destroys the foundations of all religious systems, and although in an open society most people have no religious allegiance and are absorbed in secular pursuits, there are indeed influential traditions, habits and cultural symbols that keep the dualistic notion of two worlds alive.

Humanists have no hesitation in rejecting the delusion of "dualism without," that is, the existence of an immaterial world of gods and spirits, but many are content to go along with the supposition of "dualism within": our heads accommodate two realities, a material brain and an immaterial mind or psyche, which has some ill-defined relation to the brain.

It is the purpose of this and the following chapter to dispute the idea and show that dualism within is as mistaken as dualism without.

We are thus led to an examination of psychology, and here an even more radical approach will be suggested. Of course the word explicitly describes what it is about: the study of the psyche, or, as it is more commonly known, "the mind"; but we shall ask just what it is we are talking about when we refer to this "mind".

First we may note that the mind is generally regarded as involved with mental activity, which most psychologists would agree is also a function of the brain. So in studying the one it would seem necessary also to study the other. However, it is not the structure of the brain or how it works that is the proper concern of psychologists. This is a matter for neurologists or anatomists. Psychologists look at the way the brain behaves. Thus we need not depart very far from our undertaking to deal only with simple things. The working of the brain is exceedingly complicated and not fully understood by anybody. If it were the subject matter of psychology, we should have to abandon this enquiry. But it is not. It is the behaviour of the brain, resulting in the way we conduct our lives, that demands attention, and this is relatively familiar. Although our motives, if they are subconscious, may frequently elude us, we can make allowances if we are wary; and we all know reasonably well what to expect when we are dealing with each other in social life and daily personal contacts.

Assuming, then, that psychology is the study of the behaviour of the mind, we feel justified in asking what it is we are talking about.

Readers may have noticed that up to now we have made very little reference to standard authorities in our discussion of humanism. We propose later to provide lists of sources for those who wish to consult them, but our purpose throughout is to present humanism as a natural reaction to human experience. Most people unconsciously allow themselves to absorb the culture in which they were born and reared. They are rarely stimulated to think. Thus the world over we meet with differing manifestations of cultural indoctrination. But once we realise our bondage, we do not need expert advice or learned support to discard those cultural prejudices which ensnare us. We have only to give the matter our unbiased thought to relish a reinterpretation of our experience.

However, we come now to a question, the nature of the mind, concerning which we hesitate to express views wholly at variance with tradition, without regard to those of an acknowledged expert. Having, therefore, raised the issue of "dualism within," we now seek to understand a professional exposition of the mind. In the next chapter we explore the matter further, try to trace this elusive mind and arrive at a common sense view.

So let us now divert from our stated approach and consult a book which should clarify our thinking and which, we claim, supports the contention of this chapter. The author, Gilbert Ryle, Waynflete Professor of Metaphysical Philosophy at the University of Oxford, wrote *The Concept of Mind* in 1949, and it has since been re-published by Penguin Books.

We will look first at the title. Should not an author begin by defining his terms? But the opening sentences seem to assume that the word "mind" needs no definition, and means the same to the reader as it does to the author. For he tells us that the book does not give new information about minds, but seeks to rectify the knowledge that we already possess. Thus we straight away encounter an unresolved confusion, for having used the word as though it referred to some entity – speaking of information about minds – Ryle goes on to say that he is dealing with categories of mental powers and operations. But are not these functions of the brain? Do we not think with our brains? To speak as though there were some vague duplicate of the brain, which performs its thinking, is to introduce the "ghost in the machine," which Ryle so emphatically rejects.

However, let us continue our investigation and see if we can discover what he means by "the mind." If it is not some sort of independent entity, is it another way of describing the thinking processes that occur in the brain, or is it an unnecessary concept that merely serves to confuse and impede the efforts of those who seek to understand the working of the brain?

In Chapter 1 Ryle describes what he regards as the "official" theory of the mind, derived very largely from the dualistic doctrine expounded by the 17th century French philosopher, Descartes. This asserts that the brain is a material object and the mind a separate immaterial one, but gives no clear indication how the two interact or influence each other.

This myth of a Ghost in the Machine is, according to Ryle, a category mistake. Among other illustrations he compares it to the wrong assumption that might be made by a visitor to a university, if, walking among the colleges, he enquired where the university was, expecting it to belong to the same category as the colleges.

In Chapter 2 we are left in no doubt what the mind is not, but obtain no clear answer if we continue to ask what it is. Ryle says that the purpose of the chapter is to show that when we describe people as exercising qualities of mind, we are not referring to occult episodes of which their overt acts are effects; we are referring to those overt acts and utterances themselves. This seems to imply that we are not dealing with a special entity, but with people's propensities and attitudes which result in their conduct. In fact, he goes on to say that the phrase "in the mind" can and should always be dispensed with, as it encourages the view that minds are "places". He seems to be saying that in describing the workings of a person's mind, we are not describing a set of shadowy operations. Actually, we are describing the ways in which aspects of his conduct are managed.

How, then, can Ryle continue to speak of "the mind" as though it were an entity, as he appears to do throughout the book, while at the same time denying any substance to the object of his description? For he insists that overt intelligent performances are not clues to the workings of minds. They are those workings.

Readers may care to pursue more of the contents of the book which deal with the nature of knowledge and combat the idea of the "Ghost in the Machine" in such areas as will, feeling, imagination and perception. But we consider our own purpose to be served if we cut the story short by passing on to Chapter 6. Here we give special attention to a very revealing admission, noting in passing that in Chapter 3 "the mind" is without question equated with "the soul". Ryle says that we are often told that the mind or soul has three parts, namely, Thought, Feeling and Will; that is, it functions in three modes: the Cognitive, Emotional and Conative. Interpret this as best you can, but the point to emphasize is that not only the mind, but the soul also can do without definition.

Chapter 6, then, (page 161 in the Penguin edition of 1990) contains a little noticed passage that we wish to stress. We have been looking for the meaning of the term, mind; but now we find support for our own suggestion, namely that "the mind" is a misconception, hindering study of the brain and unnecessarily mystifying us by the fallacy of dualism within. For Ryle confesses here that, although it is not always convenient to avoid the practice, there is a considerable logical hazard in using the nouns "mind" and "minds" at all. He points out that improper notions of cause and effect can follow, such as "my mind made my hand write", or "a person's body and mind interact upon each other".

All along Ryle has insisted that one's "frame of mind" merely describes one in dispositional terms. The mind is not an entity residing in the head. To say that a person is in a frame of mind to do something, is to say that he is in a mood so to act. To have emotions is to be in the mood for certain thoughts.

Our comment is to agree that thoughts are activities of the brain, not of some vague immaterial psyche. But nowhere does Ryle consistently establish this point. Several references in Chapter 5 imply that we can have a mind. If we can learn things by rational attention, we qualify for a mind. But alongside this objectification is the insistence that applying one's mind amounts to thinking what one is doing.

In the rest of the book Ryle examines various mental functions to demonstrate that the Concept of Mind eliminates the two-world theory. However, we are left with the feeling that he falls short of driving home the point and getting rid of the "Ghost in the Machine". After all, those who lay ghosts merely cause them to stop appearing. When in Chapter 7 (page 190) we read that to talk of a person's mind is to talk of his abilities and inclinations to do certain things, we can conclude that it is not a physical entity. Ryle has laid the ghost; but a humanist approach would prefer to establish the non-existence of the ghost in the first place. Instead, Chapter 10 (on the nature of psychology), seems to keep the term in unrestricted circulation, explaining that, although there are hosts of different ways in which the workings of men's minds are studied, psychology differs from all the others in trying to find the causes of these workings.

Readers may have detected some inconsistency in the use of inverted commas when "mind" or "the mind" is mentioned.

Generally speaking – it is difficult to be precise on all occasions – in this and the following chapter, inverted commas have been used when suitable. In cases where, for the purposes of discussion, we go along with the usual meaning (whatever that is), they have been omitted. But they appear when "the mind" is quoted or regarded as a misconception due to traditional dualistic ways of thinking.

TWELVE

DISPOSING OF THE MIND

So what is left for psychologists to study?

If the mind is a real thing, one might reasonably suppose that it can be defined; but it would seem that our investigations so far have led us to no positive answer to the question "What is the mind?" Even an eminent author, who should at least know what he is talking about – he seems quite satisfied that he does – has left us without a clear definition. It is indeed strange that a word used with such confidence in every-day life should so baffle us. It is stranger still that most writers seem happy to accept the word, as Ryle does in his opening sentences, without any misgivings. The view of a contemporary psychologist, known to us, is even less helpful. When asked what he thought was the best definition of the mind, he replied: "I think that asking for definitions of the form 'The mind is . . .' is a serious source of confusion. We have been led to look for this at least since the time of the Ancient Greeks, of course. However, it assumes that there is some essential ingredient to 'having a mind' and that this takes the form of a specific entity or essence. The idea that the mind is a single, identifiable entity that can exist (in principle, at least) apart from anything else lies at the very root of the mind-body problem . . ." He considered a dualistic approach inappropriate.

It is, as we have said, our contention that we are trying to define something that is not there – a difficult undertaking, like trying to define God. When people speak of the mind, they do not refer to the entity they suppose is there. It is, as Ryle says, a "category mistake." They are actually referring to something else, namely, the brain or its activities.

In this chapter we intend to accumulate more evidence for our view, and we would say to those who accuse us of labouring the point, that "the mind" may well be the last stronghold of the defenders of "another world" of immaterial entities. Further, dualism within is as much an obstacle to clear thought as dualism without.

Of all words "mind" is perhaps most prone to encourage muddled thinking, making it exceedingly vulnerable to critical examination. As we have seen, minds are supposed to be related to people's brains. For example, we regard the terms "Mastermind" and "Brain of Britain" as interchangeable. But sometimes the word is used in a vaguely generalised way, as though there were some kind of "mind-stuff" at large somewhere, and we find "mind" contrasted with matter. There is a philosophical journal entitled "Mind". What meaning can be attached to the word so used?

Psychologists and philosophers may hesitate to define the mind, but no reservations hinder the dictionaries. The *O.E.D.* gives five main meanings and upwards of twenty-one derivative ones. Among the former is "memory", as in the sentence "I will bear it in mind", and to summarise another definition, "the seat of a person's mental processes". Now these are very different concepts, and although we might accept either, it is confusing for the same word to stand for both. If mind means memory, then in the second example we are not talking about the same thing.

How can we sort the matter out? We need not be troubled, for here is another case where people are needlessly perplexed. Granted that life is full of problems and that existence itself is an inscrutable mystery, we object to unjustified multiplication of mysteries. The real problem is to understand how the brain works. As we have pointed out, we think with our brains. Thoughts are activities of brain cells, not immaterial entities. "That athlete made a fine jump" does not imply that a jump is something material or immaterial. Thoughts and jumps are activities of material bodily organs, without any independent existence of their own. They are not themselves entities.

At the very root of the confusion may lie misconceptions about the development of consciousness – that property of an animal's nervous system that enables it to react to its environment. (Perhaps the nearest we can get to a definition.) For most of the time the brain is conscious of the outside world and of its own activities. Self-consciousness is one of the most difficult concepts that we are ever likely to meet. Let the professionals apply their skills to that. But it is a matter for anatomists, neurologists, biochemists and the like, who deal with material things, not for those expecting to find some shadowy inmate of our brains. The former can trace the gradual development of consciousness as life has evolved, and, incidentally, they will not have to face the mysterious question of when mind first appeared on the living scene or whether animals have souls.

The brain too is among the most complicated objects we can possibly encounter; but, attempting to put it simply, in consciousness animal central nervous systems have evolved a far more remarkable property than is generally realised. In the case of human brains this has developed into a degree of self-consciousness that can lead to unwarranted conclusions. Our brains, being conscious of their own active processes, can give the impression that we are not just one individual, but two – observer and observed – or even several active agents in the same person. This feeling in turn easily lends support to the conception of a mind, soul or spirit – our true self, or that part of us to which may be attributed permanent existence.

Now one of the most satisfying aspects of humanism is its relevance to our actual involvement in life. Since its claims can be tested, let us suggest a practical demonstration to show that our abolition of "the mind" is consistent with the obvious facts we encounter.

As we have seen, the word "mind" is used in a number of different senses. Further, it is a very familiar word, and not a day is likely to pass without its frequent occurrence. We have only to consider such phrases as "bear it in mind", "making up one's mind", "changing one's mind" and many others. However, if we examine the actual meaning of the word in each of these cases, we shall find that it refers to the brain itself, or to the thinking processes of the brain, such as memory or decision-making. Hence for the examples we have listed we could substitute the following: "remember", "coming to a decision" and "altering one's intention". Here we are undeniably speaking in terms of brain function and describing what actually happens. Take one more example: "It is easy when I put my mind to it." What is actually happening? Clearly we mean ". . . when I think carefully about what I am doing."

It should be noted that it is not the mere word that we are seeking to supplant by putting another word or phrase of similar meaning in its place, but the concept for which the word stands: the idea that there is an entity called the mind which is connected in some undefined way with the brain or its thinking processes. Our suggestion is that "the mind" is a misconception.

Now the practical demonstration to which we referred can be undertaken as follows: try doing without the word. Wherever common speech introduces it, substitute another word or phrase that conveys most accurately the real meaning. For example, instead of "Keep an open mind", use the words "Be unbiased". After a while it will become apparent that the word is misleading or unnecessary. Let us further demonstrate this with some more cases as they come to mind (!! as we think of them!) In so doing we shall observe how the word is commonly used. This should lead to its actual meaning, if it has any.

We will put the suggested substitute in brackets after each example:

It has been on my mind.	(I have been thinking about it.)
I saw it in my mind's eye.	(I imagined it.)
The thought never crossed my mind.	(. . . never occurred to me.)
To my mind . . .	(In my opinion.)
To set one's mind at rest.	(To stop worrying.)
The balance of his mind was disturbed.	(The reasoning power of his brain was disturbed.)
To speak one's mind.	(To say what one is really thinking.)
He has a one-track mind.	(. . . always says the same thing.)
Attitude of mind.	(The O.E.D. defines "attitude of mind" as "way of thinking".)
He is seriously minded.	(He thinks seriously.)
Cast your mind back.	(Try to remember.)
He knows what I have in mind.	(. . . what my intention is.)
Give one's mind to a subject.	(Concentrate on it.)
It is all in the mind.	(One imagines it all.)
My mind was a complete blank.	(I could not think what to say.)
Great minds think alike.	(Brainy people think alike.)

Many similar expressions will readily suggest themselves. In some the mind is just another word for the brain, clearly ruling out its alleged immaterial nature, and in others it indicates some brain function. The conclusion seems indisputable: "the mind" can be discarded along with the dualistic assumption that supports it.

We can, of course, regard as harmless certain cases where the word is used as a verb. These have become so much a part of the language that we could not avoid them even if we wished, and, although they are derived from the disputed use, they do not carry its implications. So we need not quarrel with "Mind your own business!", "I do not mind if I do!", "Mind your step!", "Mind you . . ." and "Do you mind!" Further, the close association of mind with memory results in such words as remind, reminder and mindful. Here again, we need not discourage these, as they too are harmlessly embedded in the language.

Incidentally, we would do well not to reject the word "mental" along with "mind". For there seems to be no adjectival form of the word "brain" to indicate activities performed by the brain, so we have to use the noun itself and speak of brain activities. Mental could very well fulfil this function. The fact that it tends to do so already further illustrates the confusion involved in the word "mind", namely, that its adjectival correlate should regularly be used to distinguish activities of the brain from those of other parts of the body.

Indeed, it may seem unduly ruthless to exclude all uses of the term. As Ryle says, it would be inconvenient. Sometimes the alternative does not readily occur to us. "Change one's mind" is an example. "Change one's intention" seems rather clumsy, though "Have second thoughts" is effective enough. But the point is that there always is an alternative and it gives a true account of what is actually happening in the brain. Again, we may consider that the sentence "I was turning it over in my mind" loses something by becoming "I was thinking about it." Actually nothing whatever of meaning is lost, and the embellishment of the metaphor does not compensate for the confusion involved in the concept of mind. "I had a suspicion at the back of my mind" is another example: just a colourful way of saying "I was inclined to be suspicious". In fact, it is the elusive and vague nature of the mind that results in so many of the uses being frankly metaphorical. "He had half a mind to . . ." and "He has an untidy mind" are further examples. So are open and closed minds, broad and narrow minds, great and tiny minds and so forth. Even more colourful are "The mind boggles" (when we mean, still metaphorically, "The brain reels"), and "I gave him a piece of my mind."

Figurative expressions are no doubt pleasant, enlivening speech and stimulating our thoughts, but in serious discussion it is more important that we should clarify our thoughts than adorn them. It is unlikely that the problems of our time will be solved unless new lines of thought can be devised, and we shall grope towards these far more painfully than we need unless we abandon uncalled-for obscurities, which cloud the issues and serve no other purpose than to hide the real world from our view.

Let us pause here to reflect on the significance of this experiment, and consider just what it is that has taken place. We have, as we noted, outlawed not only the word, but also the concept. It is mental processes that we have encountered and these are performed by the brain itself. Just as the *O.E.D.*, in giving a definition of a word, justifies it by quoting a history of its usages, so we have tried to explore the ways in which people currently make use of the term. We might have expected some enlightenment, but if we expected to find any real entity other than the brain, our search has been fruitless.

We may note in passing the habitual association of a vital bodily organ with emotional attitudes: "He has a kind heart". "His heart is not in his work", "He died of a broken heart", "Faint heart ne'er won fair lady", "This project is near to his heart" and many more. From these expressions we might conclude that the heart is the seat of our emotions, but we would not think of doing so, as we know that here is merely a survival from earlier ways of thinking, and we would not hesitate to explain that there is no such system in operation. The heart has an essential function quite unconnected with emotion, but "the mind" has no important duty other than the one mistakenly assigned to it.

The stomach is a bodily organ as is the brain, and thinking, an activity of the brain, may be compared to digestion, which is an activity of the stomach. A surgeon can operate on the stomach, but not on the digestion, though his action may affect the digestive processes. Likewise an operation on the brain would not mean cutting up the thought processes, though it might promote or impede them.

Finally we draw our readers' attention to the way the French deal with the concept of the mind. Modern French seems to have no word that translates exactly what the English word is supposed to convey. *Esprit* is used, but it has a wide variety of meanings other than the mind. Among them are sense, understanding and intellect, not to mention spirit, ghost, soul and vital principle. Fancy, disposition, wit and character are also included. Less frequently we meet with *âme*, but this usually translates soul or spirit. Most commonly of all the French avoid the concept by changing the phraseology or employing a circumlocution:

To bear in mind:	*ne pas oublier.*
	(Not to forget.)
To alter one's mind:	*changer d'idée.*
	(Change one's idea.)
To be out of one's mind:	*avoir perdu la raison.*
	(To have lost one's reason.)
To give someone a piece of one's mind:	*dire a quelqu'un son fait.*
	(Tell someone what you think of him.)
That went out of my mind:	*cela m'est sorti de la tête*
	(Went out of my head.)
Of sound mind:	*sain d'esprit.*
	(Sound spirit.)
To be of the same mind:	*être du même avis (que).*
	(To be of the same reason.)
To be uneasy in one's mind:	*n'avoir pas l'esprit tranquille.*
	(Not to have a calm spirit.)
To call to mind:	*se rappeler.*
	(To recollect.)
I have a good mind to . . . :	*avoir bien envie de . . .*
	(To have an inclination to . . .)
To make up one's mind:	*se décider.*
	(To decide.)
To speak one's mind:	*dire sa pensée.*
	(Say one's thoughts.)
A noble mind:	*une belle âme.*
	(A beautiful soul.)

We search in vain among these examples for anything equivalent to the word "mind". Perhaps this is not surprising, as the French are careful how they express themselves.

At the best the mind is hard to find and difficult to identify when people think they have caught up with it. But we confidently go further and claim that it is in fact a conceptual error.

Humanists can approach psychology without encountering anything but brain functions. To understand the behaviour of the brain, that is, how people control their conduct, is the goal. Of course, the mind will not go away, but the use of the word will cause no confusion if we realise that it is a symbolic term for the brain or its activities.

THIRTEEN

"PEOPLE WILL NEVER CHANGE . . ."

"It never did me any harm . . ."

Religious believers confidently assert that everyone must have faith in something; so they go on to assume that humanists, disbelieving in God, cannot avoid having faith in man. Then they tell us that this is unduly optimistic, even arrogant, inviting us to look at the historical record and see what a mess we have made of our world. There have always been wars and there always will be, until we transfer our trust to God, who alone can put things right. Only God can successfully direct human behaviour. His failure to achieve this up to now is put down to sin. For God (in spite of his foreknowledge of the consequences) has given man free-will. So it has come about that man, who is helpless without God's help, cannot get it because perversely and sinfully exercising his (God given) free-will, he refuses to ask for it. Thus a ridiculous vicious circle results: the stubborn problem of evil, which, as we have pointed out, has been invented by its victims for themselves.

How refreshing it is to turn to the natural world and watch things actually happening. Natural processes (We do not need a complete understanding of them) produce changes in living organisms all the time. "Amoeba to man" would be unbelievable had it not manifestly taken place. And what about "child to adult"? People change out of all recognition in this development. They are subjected to a process known as education, and we now propose to consider it.

First, however, we must indicate what we mean by the educational system. We cannot as humanists become involved in political controversy, which asks whether the process is the same for the poor as it is for the rich. Do we not have a two-tier system? Of course we shall be unable to avoid some reference to educational practice, particularly where young children are

71

concerned, but it is the experience that most of us encounter as we grow up that we shall attend to. Education is a meaningful concept without reference to the merits of the various ways in which it is administered.

Why, then, should humanists be particularly interested in education? Apart from the fact that civilisation depends on its success, there are two very cogent reasons. We have expressed the view that we cannot take part in politics solely on the grounds that we are humanists, because we have no agreed political policy; but the case is very different with education. Here we have something to say that follows directly from the philosophy of humanism. Our view of the nature of man implies an approach which is little understood outside secular circles, and is not appreciated even by some humanists. The second reason for our interest is the damage done to children by religious indoctrination. Of course this word is not popular with those who practise it. They prefer to speak of encouraging religious awareness – not a difficult process, as young children especially will readily respond to the traditional appeal of hymns, prayers and stories.

Let us then first explain the basic difference between humanist and religious assumptions.

We have noted that as post-Darwinians we should be aware of our innate animal instincts. An animal is in general governed by two basic urges: self-preservation and self-gratification. Human beings have inherited these instincts. Anyone who doubts this should watch the reaction of a human baby if its desires are thwarted. Such protests are, of course, natural, not evil or sinful, and can by education be transformed into socially acceptable behaviour. Indeed, social urges already exist in us, but they are weak, for our ancestors were frightened and aggressive animals for a vast period of time. It is only comparatively recently that we have enjoyed the possibility of being confident and intelligent human beings.

Religious people on the other hand have supposed that we were especially created or at some stage qualified as children of God. This terminology is not so prevalent now, but its implication persists in the belief that the child will naturally display virtuous conduct if we make sure that its social inclinations are not repressed. We have observed that some humanists take a similar view, but we fear that it is a dangerous fallacy. Good behaviour must be taught and society seems to be learning this to its cost. Considerable changes have taken place in educational practice since the times when most Victorian educationalists thought that if children were given knowledge (that is, taught to read and write), they would use it to choose the policies that benefited society.

But the "progressive achievements" do not seem to have had the desired results. Youthful misbehaviour and unsatisfactory academic attainments have been alarming, and further, perhaps over-hasty, restructuring is being considered. After the unsettling upheaval of two world wars there had been much mid-century concern to improve educational theory and practice, but amid all the conferences, reports, proposals, recommendations, pamphlets and books discipline was not given a sufficiently high priority. It was allowed to slip away almost unnoticed. Even unruly scenes at sporting events have not alerted public opinion to their underlying cause, namely, the failure of the educational system to train children in good social behaviour. Young children will respond to habitual caring pressure. Now that violence is escalating in our society and schools are "fortifying" their premises, unstinted resources must be made available for the achievement of social habits.

Is it asking too much of education to train the young to behave courteously and thoughtfully in public? Is not this one of its basic functions? Why should we consider the task too difficult? It is formidable but not beyond our resources. Let those of us who despair consider our own lives. We are ordinary members of the public – protesting so bitterly about unruly teenage behaviour, but we ourselves manage to live reasonably ordered lives. We have, in fact, obtained some benefit from education. So why cannot the process succeed more widely? (We must, of course, admit as usual that we are largely free of vexatious social frustrations.)

A humanist approach to education may well improve its chances of success. Once it is conceded that children are young animals, and not young angels, the need for discipline will become apparent. However, it is self-discipline that is required, and this is unlikely to result from a return to repressive methods, such as corporal punishment, which, in any case, is now illegal.

It is good that such repression has been abolished, but a carefully considered alternative is essential. It will be motivated by affection for the children and a readiness to devote patience and understanding to their needs. Failure to achieve this productive discipline can so easily result in chaos. We have discussed the danger and few people can be unaware of it. Nevertheless we propose to drive the point home further by describing a specific example.

About the middle of the century we encountered one of the establishments set up by the Department of Education (not the Home Office) to deal with teenage boys who were in danger of becoming "young offenders". The headmaster of this school of some fifty pupils maintained a strict, though not oppressive, discipline, and administered effective educational facilities. There was an engineering department and other vocational courses as well as general education. His wife was the matron, and she dealt adequately with the boys' domestic needs. Later, however, after the headmaster's retirement, discipline slackened off, and all the efforts of social workers, who were introduced into the system, failed to restrain disorderly conduct, and the previous successful educational atmosphere no longer prevailed.

The disturbing state of education is plain for all to see. Situations similar to the above are becoming widespread, and the prevention of anti-social behaviour is increasingly difficult. In any school the key to harmonious working, constructive discipline and a good tone is in the hands of the head teacher. Only the head, by conducting assemblies, visiting classrooms and encouraging the staff, can provide the atmosphere to which children will respond. But time is necessary for this to be done, and nowadays the head is too weighed down by administrative work formerly performed by the local authority. But education plays a vital part in the survival of civilisation, and acceptable discipline is the key to its success. This conclusion follows directly from a humanist view of the nature of man. Religious views lead us astray.

As the pressures of over-population and the resulting pollution of the environment add to the demands on the emotional and intellectual resources of young people, so this humanist attitude to education becomes increasingly essential, and at the same time faces natural problems.

Like young animals, children want to play, and we see it as the role of education to take over this natural propensity, and, by inculcating self-discipline, exploit and encourage it, so that it leads to the satisfaction of effort and hard work. We have, of course, a continuing process which only formally ends when we are of age.

Play is clearly a mammalian "invention" and its function is to prepare the young for adult life. It finds little place in the largely instinctive behaviour of reptiles and birds. Their adult life does not require such preparation. And, incidentally, in humans play becomes a permanent asset and helps to sustain physical and mental health.

We have drawn attention to the disastrous results of mishandling the discipline of teenagers. This failure is based on mistakes in early years, when training in and the establishment of civilised social habits can more easily be achieved. Let us then attempt to indicate an approach to self-discipline in young children, taking up the process at the primary stage.

If not in the revealed doctrines of religion, where is moral training to be found? We suggest that human beings learn by observation and experience. Nature and human history provide parables in plenty, and teachers do not have far to seek for "sermons in stones". Let us be specific. What child will fail to ·appreciate the following lively picture? "Consider the millions of pebbles on a beach by the seaside. How stupid it would be for one of them to announce 'I am the only pebble on the beach!' Some people behave just like that and expect others to treat them as though nobody else mattered. Like the pebbles on the beach we are, of course, all very much the same. But this does not mean that we should rest content with ourselves. Look at this pebble. It is rather dull, but the sea water makes it shine. Unlike the pebble, we are alive and we can improve ourselves. To shine really well, a pebble needs to be polished, and this is hard work. The sea that made us will not polish us up. That is our responsibility, and this we can do together, helping each other to shine as brightly as we can."

Let a school motto, "My best always", for example, be supported by a deliberate and well planned course in citizenship. This will include the formation of the necessary habits of helpfulness, courtesy, concern for truth, honesty and trustworthiness. The school routine will be organised and the necessary system of rewards and sanctions carefully worked out.

A junior citizenship league could well play an important role.

We know of a school where this functioned admirably. Eleven-year-olds were encouraged to look for ways of helping other people – at home, in the neighbourhood and at school. All took to this enthusiastically, and a pleasant atmosphere resulted. On one occasion some children were observed tidying up a litter-strewn area, and when approached, they explained that they were members of the school citizenship league. A letter of appreciation reached the headmaster, who was immensely cheered, as he had more commonly received complaints about broken windows or bad behaviour.

As for the curriculum, we suggest that history is the key subject. If the future is to be happier, we must learn from the mistakes of the past. Young children readily respond to stories that illustrate the values they need to learn, and history provides endless inspirational or cautionary tales. Again we will be specific. This story takes the children back to the close of the supremacy of Greek civilisation and before the Romans became the dominant "world power." The Greek city-states portrayed excellent qualities. The Athenians, for example, were famous for cultural achievements, and the Spartans for physical fitness, but they quarrelled among themselves, and although a truce would be called to cover the period of the Olympic Games, they united very reluctantly and only with difficulty survived the Persian invasions, giving way eventually to their northern neighbour, Macedonia.

King Philip of Macedonia, so the story goes, was approached one day by a horse-dealer who offered him an exceptionally fine-looking animal. The king was interested and invited his most experienced horsemen to try it out. But they found the horse so uncontrollable that none of them could ride it, and the king was on the point of dismissing such a wild animal. However, his son, the youthful Alexander, who had been watching the display, exclaimed "I could ride it!" This angered his father. "How dare you presume to succeed where my best riders have failed?" But the prince persisted and had his way. Having been educated in Greece and trained in Greek resourcefulness, he had noticed what everyone else had overlooked: the horse was nervous of its own shadow. So he gently turned the horse to face the sun, and, leaping on its back, sped off across the plain. Fears that he would be thrown like the rest were unfounded, for it could be seen that in the distance Alexander was turning the horse and was in no danger. He arrived back in complete control of a splendid animal. So pleased was the king that he rewarded Alexander, who thus obtained his famous horse, Bucephalus.

What a magnetic personality Alexander must have had! He considered himself the champion of Greek culture and successfully led an army of Greeks and Macedonians to conquer the Persian empire. He could control animals and he could control people, but there was one person with whom he had little success: he was unable to control himself. He was obstinate and short-tempered. On one occasion he slew his best friend in a stupid quarrel. He died young because he refused to take medical advice when attacked by a fever. What might have been his achievements had he not lacked self-control!

Of course stories such as this do not display virtues that are exclusively humanist, but they show that morality can be taught independently of the divisive influence of religion. Civilised behaviour is indeed natural to human beings, but it needs to be cultivated. Basic animal instincts underlie human nature. Religious people misinterpret these as sin and introduce a seriously misguided philosophy of education.

So vital is its success that we cannot avoid engaging in an admittedly political issue: let education be a genuine national service. Should not all schools be good schools, and not allowed to compete with each other? The resources necessary to bring this about should be made available, without burdening the schools with financial problems, when their function is to teach.

Education should be a national priority, but it cannot be treated in isolation. In an unjust society, so much youthful misbehaviour is caused by frustration. Thus, as we have said, we must strive on two fronts. We need to obtain the best results amid present circumstances, but also endeavour to achieve social justice. If we do not do this, children educated to be kind and generous, will be ill-equipped for the struggles of later life.

Unfortunately, a just society may be a long-term prospect, and this makes the achievement of self-discipline so vital. Without it a chip will appear on the shoulders of those expecting the world to be lenient and to make things as easy for them as their teachers did. Social behaviour will decline and marriages will fail because family life depends on "give and take". Such an attitude is acquired by the cultivation of patience and concern for others, and will not be displayed if this has been neglected.

At the beginning of our discussion we hinted at a definition of education. The word itself, of course, comes from the Latin *educare* (to lead out). We understand this as training a person's moral and intellectual capacities. We emphasize "lead". This involves teaching, which is more than the provision of opportunities for "natural" development. We have a built-in aptitude for forming social groups, but we cannot do it free of charge. Civilisation demands self-discipline: the control of those instinctive urges we have inherited from our animal ancestors. The gist of this rather discursive chapter is to propose that humanists recognise man's situation. Religious people tend to be dominated by their supernatural commitment, and education suffers perhaps more insidiously than any other area of human activity, by being subject to the bewildering effects of various religious beliefs.

We do not of course suppose that humanist principles will immediately solve all educational problems. For example, there will be bitter opposition to attempts to introduce a secular school assembly and organise a rational approach to religion, that is, teaching children about it, rather than imposing some form of it on them. In fact, a direct attack on religion may accomplish little more than protest, and the dissension so caused will do the school no good. In such cases our approach may be more successful if we grasp positive opportunities.

The curriculum must be organised for the effective imparting of knowledge, for without it children cannot feel at home in the world or enjoy the culture we have inherited. Knowledge alone is insufficient, so at the same time they need understanding and an incentive to support that culture and contribute to it. We have suggested how this may be encouraged with young children, but it is a process that needs to be sustained. So often the enthusiasm of young children is allowed to subside, but means can be found to reveal the lasting pleasures that the experiences of later life can provide. Hobbies should be stimulated in school, and, with adequate resources to support them, they will lead to the enrichment of adult life.

Nature-study is worth suggesting. It appeals to most children, and certainly enriches later experiences. With an interest in the world of animals and plants, few people can be dull. We recall the message found in Capt. Scott's diary when rescuers reached the tent in which he and his party died, overwhelmed by a blizzard so near to safety, as they returned from reaching the South Pole. It concerned his baby son, Peter, and gave the instruction: "Interest him in natural history." Readers will not need to be reminded of the subsequent career of Sir Peter Scott. His achievement was exceptional. But for everyone an interest in the natural world may have worthwhile results. Besides providing a pleasant pastime, it may produce an awareness of the amazing diversity of animal and plant life, and so promote an understanding that we ourselves are a product of the evolutionary process.

In fact, an understanding of evolution is indispensable, and we are led to suggest that biology has more light to shed on human nature than has history. It supports us in an area where religious obscurantism may well have a damaging effect. We refer to sex education. Animals, of course, need no instruction in this, but humans do. Such is the sophistication of social behaviour. Our only concern here, however, is to point out the danger of the ambivalence of a religious attitude to sex. If this can be avoided, it should not unduly strain the resources of professional educationalists to deal with the subject satisfactorily without the aid of humanist expertise.

In this chapter we have tried to demonstrate a practical alternative to religious instruction. The obvious ill-success of the present system should be an encouragement, and we can be further stimulated by our sense of being on much firmer ground than religious people. We observe that, apart from fundamentalists few seem to know what to teach or how to teach it. Endless books, conferences, courses and television programmes clearly reveal this. Our aim is simple. We want to give children the knowledge and inspiration that will enable them to enjoy life and be good citizens. We interpret goodness in terms of human kindness. Christians are not even happy about this. On the whole they agree, but insist on bringing God into it. To be good is to obey the will of God. How very confusing we find it, and certainly no basis for successful education.

Let us again address that attitude of hope. Human intelligence has come a long way and may yet prevail, for the advantages of co-operation stand out so clearly. Perhaps we may revive the concept of a liberal education, namely, one that frees us from the bondage of dogmatic ideas and liberates our thinking. So often with hindsight we express regret for past mistakes. But, as we have said, thinking is a natural human endowment, and a liberal education should encourage it. Foresight can be achieved if children are made aware of their own nature and their place in the world. If we can but control our animal impulses, we have a fascinating and beautiful world to enjoy. We persistently criticise religion because it inhibits thought and settles for a make-believe world. Humanism challenges us to accept this world of human experience. It will fail if education is permeated by religious ideas. We have only one life to live. Let us reveal its flavour to our children and stimulate them to share in the enjoyment of the feast. We should not have a guilty feeling about happiness, any more than about discipline, which leads to it. We have to learn to live together and hand round the good things of life. We are hungry for other benefits than food. We seek mental and emotional refreshment, and preparation for this is by no means confined to school life. Our metaphor reminds us of the part played by having a meal together, such as when the family sits round the table and social training of the children is a natural procedure.

We have been concerned with school, but the home contributes no less to a child's development. Unfortunately family life is in a state as unsettled as that of education. In fact, as we have hinted, the two are related. Parents who in the middle years of the century experienced the slackening off of school discipline, are in no position to exercise control over their children. But those who question the value of the family, and wonder whether it is the best vehicle for bringing up children, should think again. Where do we find a better way? True, some advocate alternative sexual affiliations which bring them satisfaction, but children are rarely a desired asset. A bad family is, indeed, a handicap, but great benefits accrue when parents display a warm affection for each other. Their attitude is bound to rub off on the children, and parental affection for them provides security while they prepare to face life on their own.

We cannot aim too high. "My best always" may not achieve perfection, but there is no harm facing in the right direction. Children welcome a challenge. "Any fool can be a nuisance," we may tell them, but it needs some thought and determination to be good citizens.

"Be ye therefore perfect" said the chief personality in the New Testament. Unfortunately, he followed these words with a very dubious remark. . . .

Many religious people do indeed have high ideals and a crusading zeal to support them. Millions proclaim that there is one God. But such assertions seldom lead to the unity of man. Segregated schools are a more likely result. A humanist theme proclaims one world and unites mankind. This is an ideal sadly at risk when religion dominates education.

There is much concern in these disturbing times about the physical abuse of children, but they need to be protected also from damaging ideas. Because dragons and fairies do not exist, those who write stories about them will invent a world of imagination, and no one is worried over inconsistent details. But when religious people demand belief for their imaginary world, real trouble looms ahead. At best it is confusing for children to be confronted by so many competing faiths, but at worst, when these faiths conflict, bitter enmity ensues. Religious fairy stories owe their origin to alleged divine revelation, conveyed by some infallible (because divinely inspired) book, personality or prophet, and this causes trouble for us all. But the weakest in society suffer most. Children are unprotected unless education fortifies them against the myth-makers. They need both knowledge and the ability to interpret it. We have stressed the value of history. It is the field in which knowledge can be cultivated. No less essential is training in clear thought, so that the harvest may be successfully gathered in. We need to cultivate thought as well as conduct. The Greeks had a phrase for it: "Know thyself". How worthwhile is a liberal education!

FOURTEEN

REASON AND EMOTION

*Religion aggravates a conflict which is a constant
challenge to us.*

As we endeavour to replace religion by humanism, we are
frequently assured that it cannot be done because man is a
religious animal. Our answer has been that this is a
misinterpretation of human experience. In reality the religious
dimension is sufficiently accounted for by the fact that humans are
self-conscious social animals. "Spiritual" experience is social
experience derived from our consciousness of ourselves, others
and the wonders of the world. We have reminded our readers
how religion took over primitive culture in the early days of
human development, when man was ignorant of natural forces
and had no inhibitions about putting them down to supernatural
agencies.

We have further maintained that our human needs will best
find fulfilment, not in the make-belief of religion, but in the
warmth of human relationships. Religion can comfort people only
if they close their eyes to what is happening in the world. The
reasoning ability of our brains, a priceless possession acquired
during evolutionary development, must either be abandoned in
favour of faith, or misused to try to accommodate our emotional
demands. Some religious people are, indeed, able to perform this
latter exercise without intellectual discomfort, but on the whole it
is itself a stressful experience, especially for those who are
sensitive and cherish the concept of intellectual integrity.

This stress can be so severe that we propose to discuss some
further aspects of it, and particularly the damage it causes by
creating a conflict between reason and emotion.

In many ways emotion is vital for the preservation of civilised
society. It directs thoughts which would otherwise be motivated

by the need of our own preservation, towards the welfare of other people. We live together and enjoy the pleasure of mutual affection. Friendship is the cement that fortifies the structure of society. Yet we know that it is a useless simplification to suppose, like the one-time exponents of Moral Rearmament, that all would be well if we practised perfect love, for the causes of human conflict need to be addressed. There is no shortage of all that is necessary to supply human needs. With modern technology geographical obstacles could easily be overcome. The resources of the world could be fairly distributed, and the application of human reason should make this possible, but in practice emotional factors intervene. We utterly fail to reconcile reason with emotion, and it is religious prejudice that frequently blinds us in our attempt. How can we think clearly, when we cannot see the way – the paths along which so many confusing religious signposts seek to direct us?

World problems apart, it is on a personal level that religious attitudes can cause intellectual problems, especially for those who value honesty in their thoughts. An uneasy feeling is likely to arise when they seek to apply reason to their thinking; for one of the most harmful aspects of religion is its insistence on the reality of a make-believe world. The views of some psychologists are claimed in support. We are mistaken, they tell us, to assume there is a real world out there and that we have direct contact with it through our senses. Psychology, they assert, reveals this to be an illusion. What we perceive is a mental construction. Religious people readily take up this theme, and, like St. Paul, defer fearfully to the unseen spiritual forces surrounding them. But, as we have explained in an earlier chapter, common sense experience refutes all this. True, our senses may frequently mislead us, but experience corrects them and enables us to learn more about our environment and live more successfully as we do so. On the other hand, belief in some vague supernatural reality explains nothing to us and merely adds further confusion. Our ancestors were puzzled by much that we can now explain and we continue to unravel nature's mysteries; but it is unlikely that we shall ever be completely successful. An unexplained residue is bound to remain. This we should be content to accept, and not invent an omniscient god to reveal the truth and dispel human ignorance.

So much is unknown, but fear is quite unnecessary. We allow

the clerical establishment to devise what amounts to a holy protection racket, when they insist on guarding us from a danger for which they are themselves responsible. They declare we have sinned and offer to deliver us from God's retribution. but why should we be harassed and preoccupied by the fear of something that is entirely the result of human imagination? We cling to beliefs that satisfied our childish emotions, when unreasonable thoughts about a fairy world stimulated the imagination. We are in real peril, however, when fairies assume the status of Gods and take over human affairs. For entire civilisations become subject to a "one true God", who has revealed final and indisputable truth, and people are persuaded that the rules laid down by prophets in holy books have infallible divine authority, when they are, of course, wholly of human origin.

Once we accept divine revelation, we invite all the conflicts which rival faiths unleash. The religious commitments of Catholics and Protestants, or of Jews and Muslims, allow no compromise, for the truth is indisputable. Another of the terrible things about religion is its static approach, and the misplaced enthusiasm it revives for obsolete ideas. Humanism, on the other, achieves a breakthrough (at a simple but valid level) in our understanding of the imagination.

Tempered by the restraints of reason, we can appreciate more clearly than in the past the intensity of the power of man's imaginative thoughts. As we have said, it was natural for primitive peoples to suspect the presence of gods, devils or spirits in trees, mountains, streams and other natural phenomena. No doubt they met them in their dreams. They seemed real because mental processes were not understood. Incomplete as our understanding is, it is so much greater than theirs, and, we would suggest, than that of our more recent ancestors, that we face a new situation. But, to be sure, this new understanding does not impair the quality of our imaginative and emotional life. Rather, our enjoyment is heightened; for recognising our thought world for what it is, we are saved the pain and frustration suffered by those who have not attained this psychological break-through. They expect evidence of the objects of their imagination in the world of nature. They look for signs of God, building temples, churches and cathedrals, and devising all manner of elaborate religious systems in an attempt to make real what is actually a product of thought processes. In this it is perhaps fortunate that some people can achieve a certain negative success, for many are quite unable to face the prospect of the passing away of religion. We think again not only of the professionals (hosts of priests and dedicated ecclesiastical workers, not to mention their hierarchy) whose lives are wholly committed to it – we can hardly imagine what a secular world would mean to them – but also the significant number of lay people who are, for reasons we have discussed elsewhere, no less emotionally drawn to religion. They see loss of faith as a tragedy that they can ill sustain. Some blame the so-called negative approach of humanism for causing such distress, but responsibility rests entirely with those who have encouraged reliance on myths. Misrepresentation is regarded as an offence when made with ill intent, but it is no less damaging when well meant. Humanism cannot be accused of advocating a counter myth.

Some think that it may be as well that, whereas natural tragedies, such as earthquakes, hurricanes, famine and the like, cannot usually be escaped, emotional ones perhaps may; though people can avoid or rationalise distasteful thoughts only at the cost of living in an unreal world. It is a struggle which our reason continually incites, for we cannot live undisturbed in two worlds. When we realise this and experience the gratification of mental freedom, we shall not want to worry whether or not there may be a God. It becomes a matter of philosophical or intellectual interest, not emotional.

Here we think we should ask for readers' toleration when we rehearse ideas already dealt with. This is a discursive book because we seek to introduce humanism as a basically simple philosophy or attitude to life, which we acquire as our experience leads us to do so. Humanism is certainly not a set of beliefs that can be flawlessly described and enumerated. We aim to present it as a reasonable substitute for the emotional claims of religion, which will be of help to the increasing number of people who find the confusing mass of religious literature unacceptable.

Religion, then, should not be allowed to dominate our lives and put a brake on the advancement of human understanding. Man is an inquisitive animal, and an outstanding aspect of a humanist outlook is its encouragement of an objective way of thinking. We become very much alerted to the enchantment of living. Our sensitivity is not directed inwards, but we are captivated by the fascination of the world around us, leaving no desire for emotional attachment to other-worldly obsessions. Reason and emotion converge in the irresistible delights of exploring this world. The mystery of the things we see is sufficiently stimulating to absorb our attention and convince us of the futility of pursuing things we cannot see. How can we contemplate the evolution of life on this planet, with which we are so familiar, and yet about which we know so little, without an intense desire to discover more?

In the past those who have been caught up by the sheer fascination of their surroundings have done much to advance civilisation. We have already referred to the speculative brains of the Renaissance Humanists, and we can derive further inspiration from a glance at classical times, when thoughtful people were far less fettered by formal religious commitments. The attitude of the early Greek philosophers is significant. Superstition admittedly was prevalent, and the gods held sway over popular religion; but such maxims as "Know thyself" and "Nothing in excess" were expressed by philosophers whom we may truly regard as the first humanists. Reason arrived at simple statements. After all, they were not equipped with the knowledge or technology that has led modern thinkers so far beyond direct observation. Protagoras, the friend of Pericles in 5th century Athens, proclaimed "Man is the measure of all things", and typical of many Greek thinkers was the idea that man is part of nature and not the result of some special divine intervention. For a mature humanist view we may cite the much maligned Epicurus. He did not need supernatural aid in describing the good way of life. These words are attributed to him: "(It is) not possible to live pleasantly unless we also live prudently. . . ." One needs insight regarding the nature of a happy and contented life, and this will not lead to selfish actions. "Of all things which wisdom provides for the happiness of the whole life, by far the most important is friendship."

A notable characteristic of this objective love of life is the way in which both reason and emotion are equally stimulated, but these are times when the former guides and informs the latter.

Interest in our environment in place of fear is the fruit of this secularisation of thought, that is, the freeing of our ideas from supernatural ties, so that intelligent action replaces instinctive reaction. The consolations of humanism can take over those of religion, for otherwise the world can be a sad place for sensitive people. As science discloses more of the nature of the world and reason struggles to make sense of the baffling phenomena that our senses and instruments reveal, our emotions do not always keep pace. Human comfort lies in man's social nature; but in the midst of humanity we are still individuals in search of security. Literature vividly portrays this search and especially in poetry we find a revealing picture of man's hopes and fears. Poets usually possess more than normal sensitivity and many in the past have cherished and found satisfaction in religion and, of course, continue to do so. But there is always the probability that their sensitivity will lead to doubt or cynicism. Reason intervenes and emotional conflicts ensue.

At the end of the last century some poets, unable to accept the easy optimism of Victorian society, were very far from fortified by the religious faith of their time. Among them Matthew Arnold, Hardy, Housman, Swinburne and Tennyson clearly express painful doubts and misgivings. Hardy's "Darkling Thrush" portrays the mood:

"So little cause for carollings
Of such ecstatic sound
Was written on terrestrial things
Afar or nigh around,
That I could think there trembled through
His happy, good-night air
Some blessed hope whereof he knew
And I was unaware."

Of course we cannot assess a poet's sentiments from a brief quotation, but these lines from Tennyson show a similar unease:

"Break, break, break
On thy cold grey stones, O Sea!
And I would that my tongue could utter
The thoughts that arise in me."

Nor does he seem completely confident in "Crossing the Bar":

"Twilight and evening bell,
And after that the dark!
And may there be no sadness of farewell
When I embark;
For though from out our bourne of Time and Place

The flood may bear me far,
I hope to see my Pilot face to face
When I have crost the bar."

Readers of these poets will judge for themselves. What we are suggesting is that those with greatest sensitivity suffer most when they try to reconcile themselves to human destiny in the light of religion. Either they must ignore glaring inconsistencies or interpret them in such a way that renders them endurable. Both solutions reject reason and court emotional distress. On the other hand the consolation of humanism is so simple – not that it removes the need for serious thought, but, by dispelling anxiety, it invites the experience of emotional and intellectual satisfaction. It is anxiety of one kind or another that spoils life for so many people, and we think that if we have managed in this book to discover one pearl of greater value than the rest, it is this casting out of fear. Humanists rely on human affection and friendship, knowing full well that people are not perfect, but finding their tangible presence more rewarding than an intangible acquaintance with a deity. Unless we can replace religion by humanism, which means accepting the mystery of existence, our mortality and people as they are, there will always be those who suffer from the trauma expressed by those Victorian poets, though they may not describe their feelings in such moving language.

Poetry can, indeed, exert a powerful emotional effect, but it is seldom at the service of humanism. We suggest therefore that those who wish to experience its stirrings should read Housman's *The Shropshire Lad*. These poems do not denounce religious faith, but his cynical attitude condemns it and invites the modern humanist outlook which disposes of the need for religion. These verses are from a poem on the Crimean War and its effects on young recruits. It is headed "1887":

"We pledge in peace by farm and town
The Queen they served in war,
And fire the beacons up and down
The land they perished for.
'God save the Queen' we living sing,
From height to height 'tis heard;
And with the rest your voices ring.
Lads of the Fifty-third.
Oh, God will save her, fear you not:

Be you the men you've been,
Get you the sons your fathers got,
And God will save the Queen."
Poem No. 62 contains these biting words:
"Oh many a peer of England brews
Livelier liquor than the Muse,
And malt does more than Milton can
To justify God's ways to man.
Therefore, since the world has still
Much good, but much less good than ill,
And while the sun and moon endure
Luck's a chance, but troubles sure,
I'd face it as a wise man would,
And train for ill and not for good."

Here now is a poem by the scholarly and sensitive Rupert Brooke, who died during the First World War. He was not deceived by the pretences of religion. What more need "Heaven" say?

"Fish (fly-replete, in depth of June,
Dawdling away their wat'ry noon)
Ponder deep wisdom, dark or clear,
Each secret fishy hope or fear.
Fish say, they have their Stream and Pond;
But is there anything Beyond?
This life cannot be All, they swear,
For how unpleasant, if it were!
One may not doubt that, somehow, Good
Shall come of Water and of Mud;
And, sure, the reverent eye must see
A purpose in Liquidity.
We darkly know, by faith we cry,
The future is not Wholly Dry.
Mud unto mud! – Death eddies near -
Not here the appointed End, not here!
But somewhere, beyond Space and Time,
Is wetter water, slimier slime!
And there (they trust) there swimmeth One
Who swam ere rivers were begun,
Immense, of fishy form and mind,
Squamous, omnipotent, and kind;

> And under that Almighty Fin,
> The littlest fish may enter in.
> Oh! never fly conceals a hook,
> Fish say, in the Eternal Brook,
> But more than mundane weeds are there,
> And mud, celestially fair;
> Fat caterpillars drift around,
> And Paradisal grubs are found;
> Unfading moths, immortal flies,
> And the worm that never dies.
> And in that Heaven of all their wish,
> There shall be no more land, say fish . . ."

How well these verses parody the incredibility of religious wishful thinking. Emotion prompts irrational expectations, but reason dispels all hope of an afterlife, banishes religion and lays down no rules of conduct for us. Yet, as this book has tried to show, it establishes humanism, which makes possible a life worth living.

In Chapter 8 we complained of suffering a gross deception at the hands of the exponents of a spirit-haunted world, and in the next chapter we shall comment on our attempt to discover if there are, after all, any reasonable grounds for supposing that spirits exist. But before we do so, this may be the place to refer briefly to another disturbing "con" which we have not so far mentioned.

We refer to the widespread propagation of astrology. It should not be entirely omitted from a book on humanism, because it has similarities with religion. Like religion it stems from the misunderstanding of nature on the part of primitive peoples. Their ignorance of "celestial" phenomena in particular provided abundant excuses for unwarranted metaphysical conclusions. Christian believers have the Three Wise Men and the Star of Bethlehem to remind them of its ancient tradition.

One sad aspect of the situation is the fact that most of those who are responsible for the dissemination of horoscopes and other fanciful matters in the press and on television must be well aware that it is all nonsense. Their usual plea describes it as just harmless fun; but actually much damage can result when thoughtless people take the statements seriously, as they do the mistaken doctrines of religion, and organise their lives accordingly.

However, apart from serving a warning against this popular

substitute for religion (Many who never go near a church, eagerly follow horoscopes), we are not inclined to pursue the stars any further. The sophisticated defences mounted by those who abuse their talents on this very lucrative profession would demand too much tedious demystification. We cannot, however, refrain from drawing attention to just one of the flaws which undermine the whole system. Consider the assertion that, if you happen, on account of the date of your birth, to be in a position to claim association with some constellation, Leo, say, or Taurus, you are likely to portray characteristics attributed to lions or bulls. The doctrine is often played down or rarely stated as bluntly, but it is clearly a basic assumption.

FIFTEEN

THE EMPTY ROOM

Is there anybody there?

We have stressed throughout this book that humanism is a simple attitude to life. This is more than can be said of some of the doctrines that support religion.

One in particular disturbs us. We refer to an assumption that is basic to religious belief, namely, the reality of the unseen presence of God. We think that so much mystification resides in this concept, that it is reasonable to ask what it means.

In an attempt to discover whether it can be stated simply and in a meaningful way, we invited ten bishops of the Church of England (as people who should speak with authority) to give their views. A letter explaining the difficulty was sent to each of them, and six responded. All except two replied personally, and we were impressed by their sincere and friendly concern; but readers of the following unedited correspondence will judge the extent to which they have been successful in clarifying an experience which seems to humanists quite incomprehensible.

A letter sent by the author to ten bishops of the Church of England.

"As a humanist, I am seeking an answer from responsible religious people to a question that bothers me intensely.

I have been putting my thoughts together and have attempted to write a book explaining the humanist outlook to ordinary people. During the course of this I have encountered a difficulty which up to now I have found quite intractable, and I am explaining it to you in the hope, that, even if you cannot resolve it for me, you will let me know what statement concerning it seems most satisfactory to you. I cannot, as yet, discover any clear evidence of theologians even addressing the problem in terms that ordinary people can understand. I am, incidentally confining my inquiry to the Christian religion, and more specifically, to the Protestant persuasion, as I am most familiar with discussions in this context. It seems to me that we are all to some extent influenced by our cultural and religious background. I certainly feel that I have the clearest understanding when considering the tradition in which I have been brought up.

This is my difficulty. Sitting here I am aware that, apart from me, the room is empty. But the Church teaches that this is not the case. There is a "spiritual" presence in the room. God, a spiritual being, is here and moreover is aware of my presence and can communicate with me. How can this be ? How can a spiritual entity (I must leave aside the question of the meaning of such a concept) and a physical one communicate with each other? How, in fact, can a spiritual entity be conscious? Is not consciousness a function of animal nervous systems, and has it not developed over the course of evolution?

I am hoping that those who are willing to let me have their views on this matter, will allow me to quote them, so that what Christians believe may be explained by those most able to do so.

I conclude by pleading that this is a problem which ought to be faced. It seems to lead on to fundamental questions which need to be asked about the nature of God. If God is a real entity, he must surely have location, so what does a spiritual presence mean? We read that those who looked into the empty tomb were satisfied that there was no one there. Yet believers populate an empty room with this mysterious "spiritual" presence.

Unless an answer can be given, I think humanists are justified in suggesting that this is a problem that religious people invent for themselves. The ball is in their court."

Replies
Letter No. 1

The Bishop at Lambeth, the Right Reverend John Yates, having explained that the Archbishop of Canterbury was abroad, wrote as follows:

I am not a philosopher, and of course you do not ask for the opinion of the Bishop at Lambeth on the very searching question which you put. However, it does occur to me that the way you have set up the problem assumes that God, if there is one, is a spiritual being and that you yourself (or presumably any other human being) are a physical entity. Surely the religious enterprise depends upon the assumption or belief that human beings, though certainly in Christian belief physical entities, are also spiritual beings. The communication therefore that may be possible is not between the spiritual and the physical but between two spiritual entities.

Letter No. 2

This is from the Right Reverend Lord Habgood, Archbishop of York at the time.

Thank you for your letter. I think your difficulty arises through trying to think of God as a kind of entity or object comparable with other entities or objects, whereas the classic definition of God is that he is the source and ground of all existence.

I think you would be helped by reading *The Sense of God* by John Bowker, OUP 1973.

Letter No. 3

The Bishop of Liverpool, the Right Reverend David Shepperd, also replied personally:

Thank you for your letter, with its profound question. You would not expect me to write a major essay: I will try to suggest some of the directions which are helpful to me. You ask how a spiritual entity and a physical one can communicate with each other. You say that consciousness is a function of animals' nervous systems which has developed over the course of evolution.

If we begin with our experience of what people are and can be, I believe we must include words like questioning, enquiry, wonder: we have the capacity to go beyond the bounds of our own being to relate to another. I think it is fair to say that there is a "transcendence" about human beings. Transcendence means "going beyond". So the human intellect does not merely reproduce a summary of the experiences which it can define, but goes beyond them. As we go on asking further questions, I believe it would be dogmatic to assume that there is nothing beyond our rational knowing and doing.

As a Christian I believe that God the Creator comes to meet that human reaching beyond: I see the creation of the world not so much as an act of power on the part of God as his sharing the gift of existence. His creating was not simply an arbitrary act, but a caring act which sought and seeks a response: It follows from that that for Him the creation was valuable and that from the beginning he was committed to its development. The Christian story is that human beings have turned away from God: resulting from this we have denied our own possibilities, falling short of our own potential, and being estranged from one another, with us failing to form a true human community. God does not give up on us: he "plunges in more deeply" and identifies himself in a new way with his creation. "The Word became flesh. He came to dwell with us". In the Incarnation he took flesh, became one of us. As a Christian I believe that the Incarnation was not for a brief life time on earth, but that His glorified humanity was raised from the dead. His coming into the world in the person of Jesus was not some Plan B, but His insistence to the death to stand by Plan A – that he would share his gift of existence with human beings.

Communication between such a God and us can sometimes be very direct: mostly, I believe, he uses the means of grace which He has given to us both in the creation and in His entering in our world in the person of Jesus. My experience is that genuine communication with a loving Father – which of course has to be frequently tested – is part of the reality of my life.

If you want to pursue some of these thoughts, could I commend John McQuarrie's book *In Search of Humanity* (SCM Press 1982).

Letter No. 4

The Bishop of Winchester wrote thanking us for our letter, and saying that it had reached his house when he was away. He had referred it to his Residentiary Canon, who had written some interesting paragraphs, and the Bishop thought it best to share them with us just as the Canon had prepared them. He was more than happy to endorse the response put forward to the questions in our letter. Canon Keith Walker, now Librarian of Winchester Cathedral, wrote as follows:

In place of a book my answer must be brief to the important questions you ask. A Victorian poet wrote:

> "Speak to him, thou, for he hears,
> And Spirit with spirit can meet.
> Nearer is He than breathing,

Closer than hands and feet".

The essential point is contained in line two. I think you have a tendency to determine the scope of reality by what the senses perceive. Spirit cannot have location in the way a book must, though it may be more apparent to us in one place rather than another. Spirit is not apprehended by the senses. My spirit encounters Spirit and this experience is indubitable to me and to those who have a similar experience. Sherrington, the great neurologist, said he could find no explanation of mind in terms of brain. The Eternal Values of Goodness, Truth and Beauty cannot be seen physically or proved scientifically. They are self-evident truths recognised by the spirit of man. A poetic utterance of this basic truth can be found in Browning's "A Death in the Desert". A philosophical statement is contained in Paul Roubiczek's *Thinking Towards Religion*. His chapter, "Feeling as an Organ of Knowledge" would particularly interest you. He makes the point that man is gifted with intuition as well as reason and that our environment includes a spiritual as well as a physical dimension. Feeling may be a single emotion produced by a particular circumstance but it may endure and lead to the genuine knowledge of the eternal values. The martyr for truth, the artist who sustains neglect yet paints the vision he sees, the holy man dying for the sake of the oppressed are servants of perceptions intuitively and feelingly known and they recognise the authority of what they experience as more valuable than life itself.

I believe that you approach the whole subject of knowledge from too narrow a base. I believe you are a victim of reductionism or scientism. Science is good but it is only a part of knowledge. Many great scientists today acknowledge that this is so and it may be that we are entering an age when the meta-physical will be recognised as readily as the physical. If you have time to read some of the writings of John Polkinghorne I think you may be surprised. He is both a distinguished physicist and an Anglican clergyman.

Our descriptions of God are by metaphor – inadequate earthly language to symbolise the ineffable, and we never escape symbolic language in religion. This is because God is unique and inexhaustible. The early Christian Fathers had no trouble in speaking of God as incomprehensible and this is one reason why adoration is an important part of prayer. We bow before the mystery and we never explain it. The unknown author of the fourteenth century mystical writing, *The Cloud of Unknowing* says : "But only to our intellect he (God) is incomprehensible : not to our love".

In line with all this we find that biblical religion is a religion of revelation : Spirit appealing to the heart of man, his intuition and deep feeling. God discloses himself to persons in their wholeness and the Church today makes available through its ministry the revelatory moments. The record of the revelation and its guardian are the channels for its renewal.

I hope this helps a little. The questions you ask are big!

Letter No. 5

The Rev. N. Moir, Chaplain to the Bishop of St. Albans, at the time wrote as follows:

Thank you for your letter of 15 July to Bishop John. I am afraid he is not able to answer this personally but he has asked me to give you a Christian response to what you have to say.

You start off in discussion of your difficulty by saying "Sitting here I am aware that, apart from me, the room is empty". Well, that raises a host of problems in itself. What do you mean by "me"? What about the air in the room? And what does "empty" mean? On the latter point, are we talking about an absence of atoms (themselves theoretical constructs)? – but such a vacuum can still contain force fields e.g. magnetism, gravity. The fact is that when it comes down to it, modern science knows no great distinction between "matter" and "energy". In fact, the old dualisms of mind and body have collapsed into a far more integrated view of the universe. So deciding what constitutes a "spiritual entity" and what constitutes a physical one is rather more difficult than the old logical positivists assumed. I actually believe that human beings are "spiritual" in the sense that we are conscious, rational and moral beings. We live in a universe in which there is no problem communicating with other such spiritual entities i.e. other people!

But going back to your empty room, if now you put a couple who are in love inside it, does that mean that it now contains love? Obviously it is difficult to think of that on a purely material level, but we would be foolish on that basis to conclude that love does not exist. We could talk about other values and qualities in the same way – e.g. beauty, truth, joy, etc.

But I am merely hinting at some of the theological explorations that have been going on about such issues. I suggest that if you want to explore Christian theology seriously on this kind of level you should read the works of John Polkinghorne and Arthur Peacock, both eminent scientists as well as theologians.

For my own part it does not seem the least bit incongruous that an evolving universe which has the potential to produce free, rational, thinking and loving human beings also has at the heart of it one from whom all these qualities flow and in whom is the key to understanding the nature and purpose of it all.

Letter No. 6

The Right Reverend Richard Harries, Bishop of Oxford, sent us the following:

Thank you for your letter and question.

The first thing a religious believer would want to say is that God is not an object in the world of objects, nor a thing in thing in the world of things. He is not locatable, touchable, point-at-able, or anything like that. He is quite simply the ground of all being, the fount from whom moment by moment my existence flows. So to be aware of God means first of all simply being aware of one's surroundings and realising that all that is exists only because God wills it to exist. Without God all would dissolve into nothingness. He it is that holds all things in being.

Secondly, you ask how God can communicate with us. God not only holds my existence in being he touches me at the deepest point within me. He is the soul of my soul and I can converse with God who touches my spirit in this way.

So God not only moment by moment holds me in being, He enfolds me with His love in and through all that touches me and he fills me with His spirit.

Our General Impression

What can we learn from these letters? Have the bishops provided an acceptable answer to the problem of a room which is empty and yet contains a spiritual presence that they can communicate with us? They have done their best to be helpful and, as we have said, we certainly appreciate their sincere intention. But we must be honest and confess that we do not think we have received a satisfactory answer.

In fact, another basic question has arisen: we have to ask what is meant by "spirit" and "spiritual". We really need to know. Sentences such as "My spirit encounters Spirit", "I can converse with God who touches my spirit in this way" and ". . . our environment includes a spiritual as well as a physical dimension" leave this question, in our opinion, also unanswered.

We are so used to experiencing and communicating with each other in daily life, and having little difficulty in understanding what we are doing, that it is very easy to assume that we can also experience and communicate with God. But how can this be meaningfully experienced? It is conceded that human words are used symbolically, but what are they symbolic of?

A confusing picture of God emerges from these letters. Most portray a personal God, who seeks communication with us, but some speak of him as a transcendent "source and ground of all existence". How can God be both? No doubt believers will claim that God can be like a loving father (somehow imminent?) and at the same time the source of creation (somehow transcendent?); but these concepts, however they are interpreted, seem too diverse to be adequately reconciled.

Life for thoughtful people imposes a straightforward choice. Either we must come to terms with its mystery or believe in fairies (gods and spirits). In this book we have been claiming that humanism finds the former attitude both intellectually and emotionally satisfying. Our curiosity urges us to seek as much understanding as we can, nibbling away at the nut and enjoying the process, but realising that we are unlikely ever to crack it open. Appreciating and storing up whatever fragments of knowledge that can be uncovered, we accept our limitations and find contentment. As finite beings *sub specie acternitatis*, faced with the infinity of time and space, we can but ask questions, without demanding a final answer. This is the basis of humanism. The lure of religion is its claim to provide that answer: the world is God's creation; the watch-maker has been at work.

Our theme for readers to ponder is that this is mystification, and that it is futile, disturbing and unnecessary. The room is plainly empty, and no amount of theological dexterity can establish a presence able to communicate with us.

We recently encountered a clergyman who, in response to our problem, said "I don't think a scientist would regard the room as empty." We met this view in the letters and it illustrates how religious people can unintentionally mislead us by introducing irrelevant details. We all know that the room contains air and various similar entities, but the point is, of course, that none of these can communicate with us. There is no personal presence in the room. Anybody looking in would be justified in reporting that there was no one there. We have admitted that our senses can mislead us, but certainly not to the extent that we may deny their evidence and conclude that we live in a world surrounded by spiritual beings whose presence, it seems to humanists, is wholly the product of human imagination and wishful thinking.

SIXTEEN

READ IT FOR YOURSELVES

Voltaire: "Those who believe absurdities will commit atrocities."

We now ask what more can be said to alert our readers to the spurious claims of religion.

We have repeatedly stressed that humanism does not demand intimidating intellectual powers, such as those required to deal with the profundities of say, physics or mathematics. Let people think clearly, open their eyes to the evidence manifested in evolution (see Chapter 1) and recognise the emotional and traditional ramparts that defend religious belief.

But some misapprehensions call for further clarification.

In Chapter 2 we exposed the misunderstanding that was prevalent in the time of Sir Isaac Newton. Most people then accepted a deist conception of God that obscured the reality of the conflict between science and religion. In this chapter we seek to refute the common assumption that Christianity has been a pillar of support for those aspects of human conduct that cement the fabric of civilisation.

We have refrained from frequently quoting the opinions of other writers on humanism, for we see it as arising effortlessly out of the common experiences of life. On this question of morality, however, we can usefully draw attention to a book that really says it all for us.

When morality is discussed, we find very strong views expressed by people who are prejudiced by traditional attitudes which they have come to take for granted, and if they are to be influenced by new ideas, a very clear exposition is required. Having now found an eloquent and well documented piece of writing that reveals facts that cannot reasonably be denied, we are prompted to make it more widely known.

We are drawing attention to an instructive exposure of the falsity of the commonly held view that the New Testament sets up totally reliable standards for those who seek guidance on human behaviour.

First we must note that in 1963 the Bishop of Woolwich, Dr John Robinson, attempted to establish a theology less anthropomorphic than that of the Creeds and more in line with a philosophical concept of God. He entitled his book *Honest to God* and described the deity, not as a personal entity, but as the source and ground of all existence. His theme did not meet with the universal approval of the Church, but the controversy continues, as is indicated by Letters 2 and 6 in our Chapter 15. Letter 2 was written to us by an archbishop and seems to endorse Dr Robinson's views.

Nowadays, however, it is not only the actual nature of God that is questioned, but much thought is given to devising some sort of symbolic interpretation of the most intellectually embarrassing Christian doctrines, such as the Ascension and the Second Coming of Christ. We may well ask whether it is morally harmful to give these a "spiritual" significance while refraining from actually explaining them away. Unless people can be satisfied that their thinking is as honest as they know how to make it, religion will be increasingly ignored to the detriment of the morality that is tied up with it.

It is easy to manipulate the phrasing of religious statements so that they become very obscure and no one can dispute them. Perhaps there is no great harm in this. But a more serious consequence results when religious believers are misled by doctrines which they have accepted uncritically, but which are actually far from the truth.

Margaret Knight, the author we wish to recommend in this chapter, gave a series of lectures in 1955 which put the proverbial cat among the equally proverbially ecclesiastical pigeons, and led her to take up the *Honest to . . .* title and write *Honest to Man*.

In Chapter 8 we claimed that humanism, far from undermining morality, provides a powerful motive for human co-operation. Margaret Knight shows that the same cannot be said of religion, and very effectively challenges the popular misconception that the New Testament is a reliable text-book for those who wish to live a good Christian life. Her revelations may come as a shock to those who have always assumed that "the Son of God" exemplified perfection. No doubt Jesus had a number of worthy qualities. His concern for those in need of help, illustrated by the story of the Good Samaritan, and his emphasis on love and forgiveness are inspirational. But Margaret Knight points out that a careful reading of the New Testament will reveal a less attractive side to his nature.

There are passages where his conception of love falls short of that of Confucius and the Stoics, who took it for granted that man is a social animal. She reminds us that Cicero wrote "Men were born for the sake of men, that each should assist the others." And again "Those who say that regard should be had for the rights of fellow-citizens but not foreigners, would destroy the universal brotherhood of mankind." By way of contrast she quotes four sayings where the concept of rewards is attached to the moral teaching of Jesus. We repeat them here.

"Love ye your enemies, and do good, and lend, hoping nothing again; and your reward shall be great." (Luke VI, 35)

"Give and it shall be given unto you; good measure, pressed down, and shaken together, and running over." (Luke VI, 38)

"(Let) thine alms be in secret: and thy Father which seeth in secret shall reward thee openly." (Matthew VI, 4)

"The Son of Man shall come in the glory of his Father, with his angels; and then shall he reward every man according to his works." (Matthew XVI, 27)

In a section on eternal punishment, Margaret Knight cites the doctrine of hell as the most intolerable of the teachings of Jesus and the one that has had the most hideous social consequences. Of course, Jesus did not invent it, any more than he was responsible for the devils that he thought possessed people; but he accepted it and made no attempt to teach otherwise. She then expresses her relief that owing to the decline in Bible reading, few people today are entirely familiar with Jesus's statements about hell. So, she says, it will be her unpleasant duty to quote some of the more horrific of them. In case readers do not have a New Testament handy, here they are:

"The Son of Man shall send forth his angels, and they shall gather out of his Kingdom all things that offend, and them which do iniquity; and shall cast them into a furnace of fire: there shall be wailing and gnashing of teeth." (Matthew XIII, 41-42)

"Then shall he also say unto them on the left-hand, Depart from me, ye cursed, into everlasting fire, prepared for the devil and his angels . . . And these shall go away into everlasting punishment." (Matthew XXV, 41,46)

"Be not afraid of them that kill the body, and after that have no more that they can do . . . But . . . fear him which after he has killed hath the power to cast into hell; yea, I say unto you, fear him." (Luke XII, 4,5)

"He that shall blaspheme against the Holy Ghost hath never forgiveness, but is in danger of eternal damnation." (Mark III, 29)

"Whosoever shall say (to his brother) thou fool, shall be in danger of hell fire." (Matthew V, 22)

"If thy hand offend thee, cut it off: it is better for thee to enter into life maimed, than having two hands to go into hell, into the fire that shall never be quenched." (Mark IX, 43)

"Wide is the gate, and broad is the way, that leadeth to destruction, and many there be which go in thereat." Matthew XII,13)

Quotations such as these support the main contention of *Honest to Man*, which is that such blots on the record of Christianity that produced the Crusades, the Inquisition, witch-hunting, the subjection of women and other excesses, are not denials of the true faith of Christian believers but follow directly from New Testament teaching.

Moreover such acts of intolerance and persecution are indisputable historical events. No one doubts they happened. The ages of faith saw the intensity of religious enthusiasm that encouraged people to burn each other for their own good. When witch-hunting flourished at its height, between 1450 and 1550, hundreds of thousands of alleged witches were tortured and put to death. In some parts of Europe women were afraid to grow old: a fear caused by a horror invented wholly in the imagination of Christian believers.

No less appalling events have, of course, occurred in a secular context and continue to do so. Not all wars are religious ones, but the point we have emphasized here is the contrast between the assumed love of God and the outrageous beliefs, such as hell fire, proclaimed in the New Testament. We repeat: one does not have to be religious to perpetrate the horrors we have described. It is not essential to believe absurdities to commit atrocities, but it helps.

Enough must by now have been said to bring home to our readers the truth of this.

Let us summarise how Margaret Knight arrived at her conclusions. She tells us that at the time of her broadcasts, "Morals without Religion", she assumed that, although the theological content of Christianity was worthless, the moral message, as presented in the New Testament, was worth preserving. But after closer investigation, she became aware that the historical record of the conduct of the Church: its intolerance, persecutions, religious warfare, suppression of freedom of thought, other-worldly neglect of human well-being, the subjugation of women, not to mention the cult of asceticism and the condoning of slavery (which was consistently opposed by the Quakers, who declared their opposition in 1729, long before Wilberforce took up the cause) – all these things which she has so eloquently surveyed, were not a departure from New Testament teaching, but a direct consequence of putting it into practice.

Of course many of the distasteful features of the Ages of Faith, such as the burning of witches and heretics, do not apply today. But the Roman Catholic Church, battling largely on its own, still fuels the flames of hell, and the Protestant Churches though preaching milder ethics, inflict serious damage on our intellectual life by attempting to update the absurdities of Christian theology to conform with modern thought.

What are we to make of a religion that has such a mixed up attitude towards the processes on which our very survival depends? We rely on sex to reproduce ourselves, but the doctrine of the Virgin Birth implies that it is unclean. It all began with Adam and Eve. Although no longer taken seriously, the Book of Genesis explains how God inflicted painful birth on women as a punishment for Eve's sinful behaviour. What nonsense, of course, but the hangover remains. The doctrine of original sin has yet to be discarded.

Again the Catholic Church is in the vanguard of those who crusade against this major culprit among the sins of the flesh. Few these days go to the lengths of the saintly fathers of the early church. (In her chapter on the position of women, Margaret Knight quotes Tertullian, who in the 3rd century AD thought it best for a man not to touch a woman.) But obedient Catholics suffer an unhappily warped restraint on their sexual behaviour.

Gathered in the monasteries are those who regard sex as an unwelcome human necessity. That it should be a source of pleasure – well, perish the thought!

She also points out that the legend of the Virgin Birth is in line with the numerous miraculous births of the gods of Greek and Roman mythology. But most of these stories were based on the idea that a supernatural being must have a supernatural origin. It was the mechanism involved that was stressed, not the feeling that sex was shameful.

Having expressed such disapproval of the New Testament, we should not neglect to remind our readers that, although it leaves us much to be desired as a guide on moral issues, it is a source of unblemished virtue compared with the Old. Of course, few but fundamentalists admire the latter these days, but we have heard it explained that God's revelation was a progressive one. We can forget much that we read in the Old Testament. Hence the need for the New. Jesus seemed aware of this in the Sermon on the Mount, (Matthew V, 38 : "Ye have heard that it was said, An eye for an eye and a tooth for a tooth: But I say unto you. . . ."). However, the loving heavenly father of the New Testament is a blatant contradiction to the warlike God of the Old. One has only to read the Book of Joshua where God gives detailed advice to help with the destruction of Jericho. The inhabitants of this unfortunate city were in fear of their lives as the Israelite army encircled them; and not without reason, for after the mysterious collapse of the walls, all the men, women and children were slaughtered, the only survivors being a family that concealed some spies that Joshua had sent in advance.

If still in doubt about the savagery that God condoned in the Old Testament, read the Book of Kings and the Book of Chronicles in which he regularly delivered vast multitudes to be dispatched by the Israelites. Provided his people kept all the laws so meticulously detailed in Leviticus, they had nothing to fear from those already in possession of the Promised Land. The Philistines did not stand a chance. Today's video nasties, which some fear may corrupt our children, at least do not claim to be taken seriously. But the revolting biblical narratives are told as historical events which reflect the power of a jealous God, who organised so much of the slaughter. It might be well to be selective when choosing Bible stories fit for children to read.

We hope it has now become clear that religion imparts monstrous errors, involving myths and fantasies of the imagination. Some may be harmless enough, but others can lead whole communities into bitter conflicts. Realising this, humanists are saddened by the thought that enlightenment would utterly devastate the feelings of so many believers who have been indoctrinated and enjoy such comfort from their faith.

But our readers will also have learnt that there is a positive alternative to religious make-believe. It is to embrace the benefits of humanism. It is not unreasonable to do so. True, we still find in human beings the aggressive instincts we have inherited from our animal ancestors. Episodes portraying indescribable cruelty have occurred in the past and continue to disgrace us – often motivated, as we seen in this chapter, by misguided religious enthusiasm. But we are social animals. It is also in our nature to be kind, work together and pursue acts of altruism. Our future cannot be left in the hands of an imaginary God. Let us cultivate human kindness, beginning with a caring attitude to our children.

In Chapter 13 we outlined our belief in the importance of education. We must pursue it by teaching children to enjoy life, and accept its challenging demands and responsibilities, by revealing to them the fascination of the natural world of which we are a part, by giving them the knowledge that will enable them to appreciate their existence, and above all, by demonstrating good citizenship and not confusing them by basing it on incredible religious doctrines.

SEVENTEEN

THE COSMIC FAIRY

"In the beginning God ..."?

Why do some scientists believe in fairies – well, if not in any fairy, in a giant celestial one – a superbeing, in fact?

If they do not, why are a number of them – they claim an increasing number – encouraging a religious view of life?

Let us be quite clear about this. Gods resemble fairies and a supreme God still qualifies. We are entering a fairy world of confusion, make-believe and magic. But a simple proposition emerges: either there is a cosmic decision-maker, or there is not.

If we do envisage such a "spiritual" entity, "he" has all the attributes of a fairy, only more so. Fairies have the advantage of appearing and disappearing: Gods share this convenience. The Israelite God partially revealed himself in the Old Testament and the gods of the ancient world were a familiar sight. They were fairy people. They had human attributes without being tied down to human limitations – projections, in fact, of the desire for safety and success.

But should we not have grown up by now? Chapter 1 gave good reasons for disbelief, and in Chapter 9 we showed how doubtful is the concept of purpose in the universe.

In our last chapter we spoke of misapprehensions that still support religious belief and stressed how the Bible misleads us.

Now we encounter a further source of confusion, for these "Christian" scientists leave so much unexplained and the sort of religion they seem to embrace by no means ties in with mainstream religious creeds, in which a personal God is surely a prime necessity. Must we not have a God who listens to prayer, comforts the bereaved at funerals and makes his presence felt to the millions of viewers of the Sunday morning TV programmes?

But the God-conscious scientists do not speak of such a God, while yet leading us to suppose that science confirms what religious people describe as spiritual experience. This is another misapprehension and we try to deal with it in the present chapter.

We begin by asking whether it is possible to discover what sort of God, if any, these scientists are telling us about, and what justification they have for advocating religion.

Listeners to the Sunday morning church services and other religious programmes are served up with a number of varying beliefs. So in an attempt to dispose of the misapprehensions that some scientists are unloading upon us, we propose to take note of a significant but little discussed religious event at Buckingham Palace. It was the occasion of the presentation by the Duke of Edinburgh of the 1995 annual £650,000 Templeton Prize for Progress in Religion to Paul Davies, Professor of Natural Philosophy at the University of Adelaide.

That Professor Davies should be thought worthy of this prestigious award is not surprising. He is among the foremost of those scientists who claim that religion is compatible with science. But whether he wishes to follow in the footsteps of Sir Isaac Newton, we seek to discover. For most scientists in the 17th century were also theologians and considered that their discoveries revealed the handiwork of God. It is less easy to combine the two roles in these days, but here we meet one who seems to do so.

In his acceptance address at a ceremony in Westminster Abbey and in a newspaper article published on the following day, Professor Davies outlined his beliefs. Let us pause to consider them, for although he has explained his views in a number of books, what he has to say in this lecture should be a reliable summary of them.

He made it plain that he considered that the cosmic magician of popular belief (the cosmic fairy) must be discarded. He found miracles repugnant and would rather suppose that the laws of physics operate unfailingly throughout the physical world.

These are his words. Yet he seems impressed by the attitude of Newton, describing it as glimpsing, so to speak, the mind of God, as he surveys a lawlike order. This he regards as an act of faith and claims that science can proceed only if the scientist adopts an essentially theological world view.

But does it really follow? Does the existence of a lawlike order in nature necessarily imply a law-giver? Professor Davies seems to avoid a plain answer, though he is concerned to know where the laws come from, and uses the word God all the time. He reminds us that Einstein often spoke of God and wondered whether God had a choice in his creation. But one must point out that Einstein never actually defined God, and seemed to use the term as a convenient metaphor for natural processes. Incidentally, it seems odd that such a scientific genius, who envisaged relativity and space-time, should have neglected to direct his thoughts to understanding the source of it all. If God exists and is not just a product of the human imagination, one might suppose that scientists would be eager to discover all that can be known about him. Of course, there is no scientific evidence that God is real and this is an embarrassment. As for Einstein, perhaps, without any criticism of his intellect, it might be suggested that he did not feel the need to emancipate himself wholly from the powerful tradition of his cultural inheritance, which took God for granted. But not so with Professor Davies. He is not attached to any religious tradition that would motivate the acceptance of God. So we should expect him to think in an unhindered scientific way. Is it too much then to ask for a clearer explanation? He rejects the concept of a superbeing who existed before the big bang, as it begs the question of who created the superbeing. But is it not confusing to suggest that time itself came into existence with the big bang, so that there was simply no before for a God or anything else to form in? He quotes St Augustine's view that the world was made with time and not in time, thereby initiating a theological tradition that places God outside time altogether. But whatever does this mean?

Let us further peruse what Professor Davies said in his lecture and elsewhere to see if we can follow him.

Newton and his colleagues did not find science ready-made for them. There were two long-standing traditions that influenced European thought. The first was that of the Greek philosophers who reasoned about nature and considered that it was rational and mathematical. The second – we think more dubious – was the biblical notion of a historical process with a beginning and an end, based on creation.

Although Professor Davies thinks the latter a powerful tradition he regards it as a mistake to try to find God in the creation of the universe. The word "God" means so many different things that he is loath to use it. (Here at last we come to a definition.) When he does use it, he says, it is in the sense of the rational ground that underpins physical reality. God is not a person, but a timeless abstract principle that implies something like meaning or purpose behind physical existence. He thinks many modern theologians have in mind something very similar.

Indeed they do, as we can confirm from the letters in Chapter 15. But what are we to make of such an obscure conclusion? Does it really amount to progress in religion? Certainly many people yearn for a deeper meaning to life, but it seems unlikely that this will satisfy those who yearn also for something they can understand.

It may be asked who are we to dispute with such a respected scientist. But all we want to know is what it is we are meant to believe. Was Professor Davies's audience clear about it when he concluded his address by saying that he regarded the universe, not as the plaything of a capricious Deity, but as a coherent, rational, elegant and harmonious expression of a deep and purposeful meaning? But surely the purposeful meaning does imply a purpose. We are, in fact, strongly led to suppose that he finds it in "the mind of God". How can a timeless abstract purpose have a mind?

At the end of the press article to which we referred, Professor Davies rehearses his conclusions by saying that the universe can possess something like a purpose without being manipulated by a deity: a felicitous combination of time-less laws will encourage matter and energy to evolve automatically from simple and featureless origins to states of greater organisational complexity. He then admits that this is only a general trend. The details remain at the mercy of contingency. The world is thus an exquisite mix of chance and necessity.

Finally he admits also that his interpretation of nature is a far cry from the traditional religious one that places man under the watchful eye of a creator. He claims, however, that it does challenge those who hold that human life is ultimately futile because we inhabit a pointless universe. He has no idea what the universe is about, but that it is about something he has no doubt.

The mystery remains. Where do we go from here?

It has become clear that the idea that these scientists can enlighten us is another misapprehension. So we cannot do better than return to where we started. Darwin has removed the credibility of religion. It is notable that most of the scientists who beckon us towards it are not biologists. Evolution presents a powerful objection to the concept of God, as we have clearly demonstrated. Biologists can be expected to realise this because they have absorbed the wonder of the development of consciousness and intelligence. These were not there in the beginning and so cannot be attributed to God. They are exclusively properties of animal nervous systems and make no sense in any other context.

Darwin, in fact, leads us straight to humanism which really does offer a convincing and satisfying attitude to existence.We have simply to accept its mystery; striving to get to know more about it where we can. We have but to learn to live together in order to find the world a fascinating place to explore. And when the end comes, what a happier prospect we have than that of religious people! For us death brings no fear, the simple reason being that we shall know nothing about it. All sorrow will be felt by those who survive us. They have loved us and got used to our presence. So it is in life, not death, that we experience sorrow. Let us make life worth living and cherish each other while we can.

EIGHTEEN

FOOD FOR THOUGHT

SOME FURTHER REFLECTIONS ON CHAPTERS 1–17

AN ON-GOING JOURNEY.
We have tried to achieve an understanding of humanism;
but it is not a closed system with a holy book or a celestial city.
We are not pilgrims on the way to a dogmatic destination.
There is always more to learn because we are discovering about life
and continue to do so while we are living. We hope you
are enjoying the journey.

1. God and the Dinosaurs.

Religious people are fond of reminding us that the existence of God cannot be disproved. We think that it can, and this chapter is an attempt to illustrate our contention.

Perhaps we may put it this way: a rational concept of God is impossible. We are often challenged to define the sort of God in which we disbelieve. Having tried to do so, we will then be told by believers that they do not believe in that sort of God either, and they go on to give their own acceptable definition. But this invariably turns out to be acceptable only to them. Any definition of God is bound to have unreasonable anthropomorphic defects. True, some definitions, such as "the ground of our being" appear to avoid this, but their vagueness verges on meaninglessness. An inactive God is irrelevant. An active God can but behave like a human being, albeit one of inestimable perfection. He must know what he is doing. But knowledge implies sensation. Sensation implies a brain. How can God possess one? Brains have evolved in animal organisms. Up to now humanists have failed to lay sufficient stress on this fatal Darwinian conclusion. We have a Darwinian Enlightenment – a "dangerous idea" for religious people. Cf p. 134.

2.   Emotional Inducements.

Church attendance is declining and many people live secular lives contentedly and without any ill effects. Religion is seldom a subject of conversation. So were belief to be seriously threatened, it would be mainly the way of life of its professional exponents that would suffer disruption. This is largely the situation in the western world where modern technology and industrialisation have taken root. But in the Middle East and in much of Asia the social climate has remained more theocentric. Why should this be so? Why should Jews and Muslims in particular have a religious attitude so deeply embedded in their culture, resulting in its domination of their emotional lives? It does not seem to occur to a Muslim that in his insistence on one God, he needs to consider whether there is any God at all.

No doubt it is misleading to generalise, but it has been suggested that geography may indicate some partial explanation. Europe is lapped by a vast ocean which has invited exploration, and much western science has been stimulated by the needs of navigation. New worlds have encouraged new ideas. But the "ship of the desert" conveyed man over a largely static environment. It produced amazing continuity. The early civilisations in the river valleys prospered until uninformed agricultural methods turned so much of the forest into desert. The first cities appeared with written records. Architecture and science, especially mathematics, made great strides. But the sands of the desert did not lure the "ship" to new horizons and new technology to support intellectual adventure. On the other hand, the Beagle conveyed Darwin to people, places and animals that led to a re-interpretation of human history and human nature. It is significant that the scholars of Muslim universities, although they encourage science, do not seem to have much time for evolution. In theocratic societies the passing of religion would overturn the very basis of people's lives, and this emotional barrier shows little sign of crumbling.

3.   The Fear of Death.

The acceptance of our mortality is an indispensable key to human happiness. Here we have emphasised that humanism offers a very simple consideration that leads to this view. We heard recently of a young child who, having recovered from a serious operation, and having been asked if she'd feared that she would not survive, replied "Well, I wouldn't know anything about it. Would I?"

Out of the mouth of a babe came wisdom embarrassingly obvious. We need not fear what we cannot experience. Of course, having accepted this attitude, we have had to admit that the circumstances prior to death can be exceedingly unpleasant, but medical technology is becoming increasingly helpful, and humanism enables us to be mentally prepared for the inevitable event.

The humanist view of death, though simple and satisfying, is a revolutionary breakthrough in the context of normal belief. Let us cherish it, for if we understand that no further existence awaits us, we are the more strongly motivated to make the best of the life we have.

Although the assumptions of religion concerning "life after death" do not stand up to rational thought, they are still widely endorsed. This can be only because they are largely ignored until the occasion arises, and are then formally recited by priests at funerals. It is to be noted, however, that people find these occasions increasingly disturbing, and it is not surprising that many are asking for secular arrangements to replace them. At the end of this book we mention an organisation that can be approached by those wishing for a non-religious ceremony.

4. Happiness and Sense Experience.

When we claim that only material things exist, much confusion arises because people fail to distinguish between "things" and their activities – between matter and motion. We gave an example, pointing out that the jump made by an athlete is an activity of a material person. Of course the jump exists in the sense that it happens, but not in the sense that material things exist. Here philosophically inclined readers may complain that we are stating a mere truism, as we seem to define "things" and "exist" in terms that imply each other. Descartes, however, was no less guilty in asserting "I think, therefore I am." The use of the first "I" itself implies its existence. Our point is, of course, that religious people mistakenly accept the existence of non-material things.

The issue could very well be complicated beyond the understanding of most of us if we listened to what some physicists say about entities with no mass. But this is irrelevant to the simple fact that in every-day life – the life so important to each of us – materialism is a common-sense view. If we think about it, disregarding the doctrinaire pressures of religion, we realise that it has nothing to do with conduct, but is a philosophical interpretation of the nature of the "material" world.

Incidentally, we have come across some more uncomplimentary descriptions of materialism which religious people have thought fit to apply. These include naked, dreary, ruthless, brutal and bleak.

5.   Why, then, Does Religion Still Survive?

We have stressed that far from solving the riddle of existence, religion merely adds a further mystery. Yet the feeling of its relevance persists and is frequently the first reaction when the question of the origin of the universe is raised. "Surely it did not just happen!" And believers are quick to point out that some physicists support this mystical approach. Religious people also note the failure of scientists to come up with a clear-cut explanation of their own. We do not think it was unfair to suggest that their "official" account of the beginning in terms of a "big bang" may be regarded as a sort of scientific Genesis, for it does not appear to provide any plausible indication of the circumstances that caused the initial explosion. But there seems little doubt that many people are impressed when not only highly qualified academics, but also respected public figures manage to walk a tightrope in these matters. By a skilful balancing act they hold up belief and present it in a way they claim does not offend intellectual integrity. And, of course, the very vagueness of the concept of God enables people to invent their own theologies. We see these blossoming in the various cults that are becoming more numerous than ever. Perhaps no less attractive are the emotional enticements of evangelical movements and the enthusiasm of born-again Christians.

In writing about humanism we have tried to keep our thoughts simple, for most issues can be easily understood; but we must admit that some are complex. These include the survival of religion, and we cannot hope to cover all aspects that need to be considered.

Perhaps we should ask whether religion performs a biological function that gives it survival value. In so doing, we must realise that its manifestation world-wide lacks uniformity. Many strands combine to produce the observed results, so some generalisations must be allowed. After all, if worthless, they can be discarded, but if suggestive, may be left for those more competent to develop.

In early times when humans lived in family or tribal groups, competition was intense and religion clearly had a biological function. It encouraged people to multiply and, as they became farmers, ensured the fertility of crops and animals. Nowadays its biological function is less clear. It tends to regard sex for pleasure as a sin, confining reproduction strictly within marriage.

But as modern industrial society has developed, the social function of religion seems to have become dominant. We have already dwelt on its alleged support for morality. To this we need to add its contribution to social stability, that is, the maintenance of the existing structure of society. As the owners of factories and estates prospered, those whose labour needed to be exploited were tamed by religion. "Spiritual" songs helped to pacify the slave population of America and the Wesleyan Methodists inspired love and hymn-singing rather than protests against unjust conditions. Incidentally, benevolent owners of wealth could obtain a comforting bonus by selective deeds of charity.

The scenery has changed, but religion has not left the stage – still declaiming well known lines and learning new ones all the time.

6. Morality at Risk?

We think we should draw attention yet again to the fact that morality calls for social justice. It is asking a lot to expect exemplary behaviour from those below, on or near the poverty line, or from the inhabitants of our cardboard cities.

Humanists are often expected to have a social policy that will lead to fair shares for all. But this is a political issue and progress must be in the hands of all people of good will. Most of us agree that parliamentary democracy is the best vehicle for change, but the task is indeed formidable. Over-population has caused enormous problems. Everyone cannot own a car, to name an obvious example, for there would neither be room on the roads, nor would the air be fit to breathe. Who then should have the privilege? At present those who can afford it, and there seems little alternative to this economic "free for all": a scramble which is likely to result in riots and social disruption.

How easy it is to state the difficulty, but clearly, if civilisation is to survive, a moral solution must be found. It is, however, a human problem and has to be approached in human terms. So often in the past religion has been used to bolster up the powerful. The "divine right of kings" has long since lost credibility, but now, together with the authority of God, that of any all-powerful human rulers may well be increasingly called into question. In this way, it has been suggested, humanism has prepared the ground for democracy.

7.   Civilisation at Risk

Kenneth Clark disavowed humanism on the grounds that he did not disbelieve entirely in the supernatural.

Perhaps we may take this opportunity to ask "If religion is associated with the supernatural, at what point does it depart from superstition?" The *Oxford English Dictionary* defines the latter as, among other things, "credulity regarding the supernatural". We understand this as belief that the supernatural manifests itself in the world of the natural. To suggest that any form of religion is superstition would, of course, be strongly contested by all religious people. But would their protest be justified, for they cannot deny their widespread belief that God influences or intervenes in human affairs? Unless the "deus" who started the whole thing off is also the "theos" who keeps it going, his presence can be ignored. No doubt theologians will continue to ponder this problem which they have invented for themselves.

8.   Living Together.

The assertion that the fatherhood of God implies the brotherhood of man is one of the most misleading claims of religion. Only as sons of man can we have any hope of realising human co-operation.

Ever since the one God emerged from the ancient world of gods and goddesses, the concept of the divine family has been a stumbling block to thoughtful people. Of course the sexual aspects of the godhead have become purely symbolic, but as such they are open to conflicting interpretations which have divided, rather than unified, mankind. Successful living together is a wholly secular exercise.

9. Has Life any Purpose?

To furnish God with a personality and set him participating in human affairs results in tragic dilemmas which cannot be intellectually sustained. Far from making sense, a divine purpose defies all reasonable interpretation. We think of a thanksgiving service held after an accident at sea. All the crew and passengers (the latter mostly children and their teachers) were saved – all, that is, except two: one teacher and one child. What happened to them? Was this God's carelessness? Such painful speculations have to be ignored by the faithful if God's reputation is to survive intact. He is thanked for good harvests, but never blamed for bad ones.

10. Approaching the Question: "Do we have free choice?"

It would probably be generally agreed that our most persuasive sensation of freedom is in our thought processes. We choose what we will think. It is when we come to plan activities and implement our thoughts that the restraints upon us become obvious. A hermit in isolation would still be subject to the forces of nature, and the very absence of other people would restrict his choices. Living in society, we feel that we can think what we like, but our freedom of expression is limited. The common-sense view would seem to be that our freedom is indeed partial, but that we have sufficient to be satisfied that we are actors in the drama of life and not just puppets. That freedom is a total illusion becomes a purely theoretical speculation and need have no practical consequences.

That over-all feeling of freedom that we experience most of the time is seldom considered in discussions on determinism. But it is the key to a fulfilling acceptance of our human condition. Of course as we have said, we cannot expect to be completely satisfied and suppose we have solved this elusive philosophical riddle. Our experiences are a mixture of chance and necessity, the end result being an over-all feeling of freedom. Let us not hesitate to accept it and, against the background of the mystery of existence, respond to our natural instinct to make life worth living.

11. & 12. On Psychology.

Elsewhere we have evaded involvement in the profound mystery of the world around us, maintaining that the simplicity of a humanist attitude is all that is needed for a satisfying interpretation of human life. Here we have similarly dismissed the necessity of unravelling the equally obscure nature of the world within us. We have seen how psychologists become immersed in the pursuit of an imaginary "psyche", supposing that they will reach an understanding of mental phenomena. There is but one problem, namely, how the brain works. Mental events are brain events and their explanation is more appropriately in the hands of anatomists and neurologists, who so far have much to discover. The nature of memory, for example, is far from completely understood, and it seems unlikely that computer simulations will clarify it. In fact whole books can be written on the way memory behaves, without even considering how mental experiences can be stored in the brain – what they are, where they are and how they can revive the sensation of the original input.

Meanwhile, however, in exposing the imaginary nature of "psychic" phenomena, in eradicating dualism from psychology, we have disposed of an area which religious people increasingly favour as a site where our "soul" or "spirit" is likely to reside.

13. Education.

We have been tempted to claim that education should be a public service, laid on like other public facilities such as water (in the past), policing, fire-fighting and the Health Service. It should not be put up for sale, because all children must have it, regardless of their parents' ability to pay. They need it in their own right and should not have to compete for its benefits. We would beg that this be regarded as an area of social responsibility where humanists should take a firm stand: an attitude which follows from our post-Darwinian insight regarding the nature of human development. It is necessary to train and socialise youthful human behaviour. The aggressive instincts of our animal ancestors are present in us. We should not need to be reminded of this.

14. Reason and Emotion.

In a word, humanism leads to a new understanding of human nature. It cannot, of course, be complete. We have to accept the mystery of our existence. What is new is the realisation that it is natural processes, inscrutable as they are, that have produced and sustain us.

Our remote human ancestors inherited animal instincts that equipped them for survival. Intelligence gradually evolved and reason was able to restrain emotion and combat fear and misapprehension; but only slowly have we realised the objectivity of nature, that is to say, that only living animal organisms can behave purposefully. Religion preserves the fallacy that nature harbours subjective forces: gods and spirits that are supernatural and yet manifest themselves in the natural world.

We are reminded of Ruskin's term "Pathetic Fallacy": the transference to external objects of the spectator's own emotions. He was, of course, a deeply religious man, and used the expression in relation to the feelings of artists. But we may appropriately borrow it and apply it to the religious attitude to nature, for ever since the beginning of human self-awareness religious systems have tried to accommodate supernatural beings within the framework of the natural, furnishing them with human intelligence and emotions. But it is an illusion. Human beings have a monopoly of human behaviour.

No divine intelligence can account for the world of our experience. The mystery must remain. After all, in the context of infinity, human investigations can but relate to local circumstances. We should be foolish to imagine that any suppositions can embrace ultimate validity.

Against the background of infinity, indeed, does anything matter at all? We answer that it matters to us. Emotional reactions to our human situation effect our enjoyment of life, even more than the possession of a secure livelihood, though the latter, as we have repeatedly insisted, is for most people a vital necessity. It is natural for us to reason about the circumstances of our existence, and when we come up against speculations concerning the nature of God, we find some of the more ridiculous of them outrageous and offensive. We are often lectured about disturbing the feelings of sensitive believers, but we seldom hear of the intellectual insults suffered by non-believers. Perhaps the crudest of these is being asked to suppose that God is a real entity, who is a personal God and concerned about our well-being, and yet omnipresent. How can a real entity exist in two or more places at once? Of course it cannot. Plain common-sense and everyday experience tell us this, and if they are to be denied, there must be a very good reason. Religion fails to supply one, but involves us in a self-inflicted problem, motivated entirely by emotional attitudes. We need not endure it. If our readers can be shown that religious experience is a very sad delusion, kept alive not only by our supposed need for it, but also by the understandable arguments of those with vested interests, this book will have achieved some useful purpose.

15.   The Empty Room.

We have already referred to the outrageous deception that has beset mankind from primitive times, namely, that "spiritual" entities share our world and can communicate with us. This, of course, is not a deliberate deception. Its perpetrators – the clerical establishment and their sympathisers – deceive themselves. Our hope is that people will at last recognise that the room is empty and that the alleged spiritual occupants are the result of self-delusion largely due to social conditioning. The mystifying words and contradictory statements occurring in these letters, should reveal quite plainly that the exponents of religious doctrines have no agreed solution to the problems that these doctrines present.

The authors of the letters are influential churchmen and would be expected to clarify what the church teaches. One, indeed, is an Archbishop and his words reveal how modern religious thinkers are struggling to present a less anthropomorphic concept of God. We refer to letter No. 2 in which we are told that the classic definition of God is that he is the source and ground of all existence. This description must surely mean the abolition of the Lord's Prayer. For it implies a non-personal God, very different from the heavenly father whom Jesus portrayed as so concerned about the welfare of each one of us. How can the Church have it both ways?

16.   Read it for Yourselves.

When the foundations of a religion are based on a holy book, they can so easily also support a ruthless attitude that crushes free-thought and imposes a puritanical influence on education and many other aspects of people's lives. Western society is fortunate in being largely free of the fundamentalism which at its worst can dominate an entire national culture.

We value a positive outlook on life, but we do well to announce ourselves firmly as anti-revelationists.

17. A Cosmic Fairy?

We have noted that most of the scientists who want to interest us in religion are not biologists. But as physicists they seem quite happy to give a biological description of God. It is unlikely that many biologists would be prepared to do this, fully realising the biological implications of consciousness and intelligence.

Religious people often claim that scientists need faith when they assume that the laws of physics are not arbitrary, but manifest nature's rationality. But no such faith is involved. All scientific conclusions are provisional. It is religion that leaves no room for uncertainty. How can a scientist encourage it?

NINETEEN

IN CONCLUSION . . .

Responding to Humanism

As a summary of the main themes of this book, we append the following:

A talk given by the Author to introduce a discussion on humanism at a public meeting organised by a group affiliated to the British Humanist Association.

We address ourselves mainly to those who are concerned to discover a satisfactory philosophy of life. Many people seem uninterested, or are prepared to associate themselves vaguely with the traditional beliefs they have inherited. We think that what we believe is important. The reasons for this I will make clear later.

Large numbers of those who have this concern, that is, to find a satisfying philosophy of life, adopt some kind of religious attitude; and owing to the historical and geographical circumstances that apply in this country, the great majority will endorse some kind of Christian belief.

Now, in our view, humanism produces a far more satisfactory attitude to life than any religious persuasion, and for the purpose of our discussion this evening, I want to outline three specific challenges which humanism offers to a religious view of life:

1. An intellectual challenge.
2. An emotional challenge.
3. A social challenge.

1. The Intellectual Challenge.

Humanists do not, of course, claim to be more intelligent than religious people, for there is no need to be highly intelligent to understand humanism, which is, indeed, a simple system of thought. I refer now to the intellectual aspect merely by way of contrast to the emotional one. I wish first to deal with the way we think about these matters. I begin, then, by defining humanism. Briefly, it is a human-centred attitude to life. Humans are products of natural processes: millions of years of evolutionary development. Along with other animal organisms, we find ourselves conscious subjects in an objective world. In addition we have developed self-consciousness, so that we can look at ourselves as well as the rest of nature. Nature itself, however, is objective. There is but one world of subjective activity. We are aware of no effective self-conscious entities other than ourselves.

In contrast to this, religious people seem to believe in two worlds: the world of sense (the material world,) and the world of non-sense (inhabited by spiritual or supernatural beings.)

The humanist challenge consists in this: the utter impossibility of an intelligent concept of God. We are told that psychology is a young science, which has yet to provide a mass of agreed factual statements like those of some other sciences. But one thing it should make very clear. Consciousness has evolved along with animal nervous systems. It has not produced itself. It has not entered into life, but has evolved and is a function of animal organisms. Over the course of evolution we see various stages of its development.

Now let us consider this carefully, because it implies that there can be no consciousness apart from living organisms which manifest it.

Here, of course, is the point: however God is defined, God must be a conscious agent. But we cannot conceive of a disembodied consciousness – not if we are to preserve intellectual integrity. To speak of some force of a spiritual or non-material nature, which "embodies" a kind of consciousness, is merely to use meaningless words. Existence remains a mystery. We do not solve it by introducing a further mystery, namely, some supernatural designer.

2. The Emotional Challenge.

Humanism is a positive alternative to religion, but it is a very radical alternative, and the power of the emotional barrier in the way of its acceptance is seldom recognised. Put yourself in the place of a professional member of a religious organisation. Most members of religious hierarchies are sincere, warm-hearted people. They are committed to working for human welfare. They will claim that they serve God rather than man, but they actually measure their success by what they do to help man. Many devote their lives unselfishly to human welfare. No one willingly accepts that this sort of life-work is based on an illusion. Thus many intelligent Christians employ their intelligence to think of reasons for believing what they want to believe – or they fall back on faith, which is "the assurance of things hoped for." They are not insincere, but victims of emotional stress. They are emotionally committed: arguing against humanism much as a butcher argues against vegetarianism.

The emotionally committed are not only those who have an economic or professional stake in religion. The saddest cases are found among ordinary members of religious bodies who have been brought up to rely on otherworldly support. Especially in times of bereavement such people cling to the stories they have been told. What a pitiful sight this is, and so very unnecessary, for a humanist view of death can completely liberate us from the anxieties normally involved therein. A humanist need have no fear of death because he knows that death can never be experienced. How can we fear something we shall never know? We cannot *be* dead. Just as we had no complaints before we existed, so we shall have none after. Thus, if we accept the emotional challenge of humanism, we find ourselves in a very rewarding situation. No longer do we suffer such a painful clash between reason and emotion. Trying to live in two contradictory worlds puts an intolerable strain upon people. They search desperately for signs of God in the real world, building elaborate temples and religious systems in an effort to convince themselves of the reality of what is actually a figment of their imaginations. It is so easy to *think* of God, just as we think of dragons and fairies, but we shall not find them in our real experience. This brings me to

3.   The Social Challenge.

For if there is no God to help us, clearly we must help each other. In bereavement we must comfort each other, and this, of course, we do quite naturally – and more effectively if unembarrassed by a divine comforter. It is in our nature as social beings to share each other's burdens, and try to make society such that each member will feel at home and secure.

Only humanism offers a basis for uniting mankind. Religion does the reverse. It separates man from man and threatens the very existence of civilisation. I said at the beginning that humanists consider that what we believe is important. If you doubt this, look at those areas of the world where bitter strife is occasioned by religious rivalry. The sub-continent of India was divided up into hostile states purely on religious grounds, and no one needs to be reminded of the situation in Ireland. Religion encourages some nations to regard themselves as special people, and they cannot easily tolerate other religions.

The terrible thing about religious conflict is that there can be no compromise, no solution. Heretics are no longer burnt alive for their own good, but bullets and bombs still serve the interests of religious intolerance. Annihilation seems the only alternative to conversion. Political and economic conflicts can, with goodwill, be solved, because we know what they are about. Religious disputes are insoluble, because nobody knows what they are about. Religious concepts, being products of the imagination, can be as variously interpreted as there are various protagonists.

But, you may ask, what of the good that religion does and has done? The plain fact is that you do not need to be religious to be friendly, loving and peaceful: but you do need to be religious to portray religious emotions which result in such ruthless denial of all humane affections.

So there it is. We want to put it to you that we should be true to our actual experience of life. We experience the people and things around us. If there is any reality inaccessible to our senses, how can we know anything about it? We can, of course, think about it, but we actually live in one world – the world of sense experience. It is the only intelligible world, and this would be obvious but for the emotional inducements I have described. It seems to us that we must act intelligently and emotionally in a way that will mitigate to some extent the disastrous social consequences that are inseparable from a religious view of life.

BOOKS AND OTHER INFORMATION

Postscript 1

We found Kenneth Clark's *Civilisation* a useful source for the historical interpretation of humanism. With its description of the Renaissance period it provided a setting for the ideas that subsequently developed.

Gilbert Ryle's *The Concept of Mind* cleared the way for the removal of an immaterial occupant of our brains. We now mention *The Unnatural Nature of Science* by Professor Lewis Wolpert, because it ties in well with the theme of this book. It reminds us that common sense, interpreted as "natural thinking", has little place in understanding the complexities of science. This we offer as one explanation of the fact that, although religion is incompatible with science, many scientists are deeply religious. Humanists should enjoy the enlightening discussion of the nature of "unnatural thinking": the special kind of thinking which Lewis Wolpert claims is necessary for science.

We have referred to the way in which some Victorian poets illustrated the anxiety aroused in sensitive people by the decline of religious faith. Among them was Matthew Arnold whose poem "Dover Beach" contained a metaphorical description of this decline: "the melancholy, long withdrawing roar of the *Sea of Faith*". (italics added) This expression has recently been taken up by a group of Church of England members in an effort to establish an intellectually responsible version of the Christian religion. The movement centres round the writings of Don Cupitt of Emmanuel College, Cambridge, who broadcast a series of television pro-grammes, entitled "The Sea of Faith" which were published by the BBC in 1984. Readers will find in these lectures a very eloquent survey of the issues dealt with in this book. Incidentally, we are sad to note that the clerical hierarchy wisely ignore this very competent scholar, while showing themselves prepared to take stern measures against the less influential of their wayward clerics. Indeed although long term optimism survives, orthodox religion remains firmly established worldwide.

A further disturbing aspect of our times is the success with which some scientists (mostly physicists) are coming to the rescue of religion. We have featured the efforts of Paul Davies. Any reader prepared to sort out some rather conflicting and, it might be suggested, unscientific ideas, may be interested in one of his many books, *The Mind of God*, (published by Simon and Schuster in 1992). Freely using the term God, he yet seems to want to envisage design in the universe without a personal designer. His conclusions do not remotely support the Christian faith of the New Testament, but are sufficiently encouraging to those who maintain that science does not conflict with religion, for them to open the door of their spiritual fold. He has not declined to enter. Is he prepared to lodge there, and, like the scientists of Newton's day, become a theologian? Some of his colleagues have taken up permanent residence. As we have said, although long-term optimism is justified, orthodox religion remains firmly established so far. Pensioning off the Pope will have to be postponed. It is quite unthinkable for the time being.

Meanwhile those wishing to support humanism can choose from four organisations, all integrated and separated mainly by historical circumstances. Here are brief quotations from their statements of aims:

The British Humanist Association (BHA) is concerned with moral issues from a non-religious viewpoint and with the achievement of a more open, just and caring society. It is not anti-religious as such, but seeks to put an alternative moral view of current and social issues. Bi-monthly journal: *Humanist News*.

The National Secular Society (NSS) is the leading militant organisation in the freethought movement, acting as a sort of trade union for unbelievers in the face of religious privilege and the survival of superstition. Monthly Journal: *The Freethinker*.

The Rationalist Press Association's (RPA) particular contribution to the humanist movement is as a publishing organisation, producing magazines, books, pamphlets and leaflets on all subjects of interest to the general cause of freethought. Its distinctive feature is its commitment to the principles of rationalism – defined as the mental attitude which accepts the primacy of reason and aims at establishing a system of philosophy and ethics verifiable by experience and independent of all arbitrary assumptions or authority. Quarterly journal: *The New Humanist*.

All these are based at Bradlaugh House, 47 Theobald's Road, London WC1X 8SP.

Fourthly, the South Place Ethical Society (SPES) at Conway Hall, Red Lion Square, London WC1 4RL, is a cultural and social organisation whose chief objects are the study and dissemination of ethical principles, the cultivation of a rational and humane way of life, and the advancement of education in fields relevant to these objects. Monthly journal: *The Ethical Record*.

The provision of humanist ceremonies on the occasions of births, marriages and deaths is organised by the BHA from whom the following booklets describing facilities may be obtained:

> *New Arrivals*
> *To Love and to Cherish*
> *Funerals Without God*

The BHA also supplies:

> *Coping with Death* by Leslie Scrase

A booklet by Barbara Smoker entitled "Humanism" is available from the National Secular Society, and the following are on offer from the RPA:

> *What is the Bible?* by Carl Lofmark
> *Does God Exist?* by Carl Lofmark
> *Humanist Anthology* by Margaret Knight, (revised by Jim Herrick, August 1995)

Also from Prometheus Press (UK agent Mr M Hutchinson, 10 Crescent View, Loughton, Essex LG10 4PZ):

> *In Defence of Secular Humanism* by Paul Kurtz
> *Foundations of Humanism* j121

Postscript 2
Some Concluding Reflections

Humanists, having shed the make-belief of religion, have no mental obstacles to feeling at home in the world, and can come to terms emotionally with human mortality.

Happiness is possible, and humanism helps to make it so. Our book has tried to put this clearly. If we have succeeded, perhaps its literary and structural shortcomings may be forgiven.

After all, if we can accept our mortality, the fear of death will go away, and what a great benefit for us! Religious people should be envious. For amid all the uncertainties of human life, one thing is completely certain. We shall all die!

Furthermore, it is no less certain that the earth will not support life for ever. (How do religious people deal with this?)

So the sociobiological equation, as perhaps we may call it, suggested on page vi needs these words added: ("while cosmic conditions permit").

The inevitable long-term end is not a present concern for humanists, but religious believers should encounter problems, unless a whole new mythology can be invented.

Postscript 3

We have stressed that not only should mythology be discarded, we must also face up to a realistic view of human nature: a Darwinian view. If we do so, we may not be unduly depressed. For although our remote ancestors were animals , and only over the last million years or so have human characteristics of co-operation and mutual support evolved, these attributes have indeed emerged and the process continues. It has been a gradual development, but presents a far from gloomy picture. We see the early stages of human social instincts in apes and kindred animals, as Sir David Attenborough, David Bellamy and many other naturalists so ingeniously demonstrate on television. Moreover, as we pointed out, a measure of intelligence is at our disposal, and along with our social attributes has rewarded us with civilisation. Certainly it is precarious. A thin line separates it from chaos, for many human activities are grossly uncivilised; but this intelligence has produced technology and may yet make it obvious to us that we cannot survive without friendship and goodwill. It may tame the urge for individual self-preservation which is a basic instinct, and can so easily lead to greed, making the organisation of economic processes impossible.

Along with social feelings we seem to also to have developed certain cultural enthusiasms which help to divert and control our aggressive instincts. The challenge of sport, an inquisitive interest in the revelations of science, the practice of art and the search for beautiful things, even the development of a sense of humour – all these point in the same direction: the civilised aspects of human nature. In Chapter 13 we laid great emphasis on the value of education (where, incidentally, the misapprehensions of religion can do so much harm), for properly administered, it can help us to appreciate these various activities. We suggested a motto for children: "My best always". In adult terms this may lead to a commitment to excellence. There is that within us which strives towards perfection, and we admire those who excel in achieving it. Aiming at hitting the bull's-eye, the very centre of the target in marksmanship, has widespread fascination. Consider the stories of David and Goliath, Robin Hood, and William Tell, not to mention high scoring in snooker expertise. All these aspirations are grounds for optimism, for they reveal our basic urge to reach the summit of human ability. Education should support, fortify and inspire progress.

Are not humanists, then, people with a mission? We seek to cultivate human social instincts. We must, of course, beware of claiming a monopoly of wisdom. Many who conscientiously make their living out of religion, aspire to promoting human betterment, and advocate well-considered solutions to social problems; but their basic assumption of the existence of a personal, caring and all-powerful God, who will assist in their endeavours, must be exposed as an illusion. The realisation of this opens the door to human effort. No supernatural back-up is available.

There are, of course, some who cynically cast doubts on the merits of those who have a vision. They take a pessimistic view of the prospect of progress. We could urge such to reflect on history. Once human beings lived in caves or shelters, constantly in fear of evil spirits and the malignant forces of nature. More recently they have burnt various heretics and witches, and enslaved their fellow humans into bondage. If such practices are still not entirely ended, there has been a marked diminution in their excesses, and on the whole people live longer and will, we hope, inhabit a safer world in the third millennium. This book maintains that humanism inspires us to use all our emotional, physical, moral and mental resources in the service of our species. (Let us omit the word "spiritual" from this list. We should not borrow the term from religious people, however much they encourage us to take it over; for all their other-worldly assumptions are implied in it.)

Humanist hope is so much more realistic than religious faith. We have a vision that is not beyond human achievement, and is so inspirational that we respond to the very potent urge within us to climb to the heights. This analogy is no misleading metaphor. Climbers aspire to conquer real mountains, giving us the reason "because they are there". Of course they are there, but the need to climb them arises because of a compulsive human desire for achievement. We seek no reward in a fictitious world-to-come. In death sensation ceases, but meanwhile the experiences of our brief life on the mountain slopes can satisfy our nature.

Not all of us are fortunate in having adequate health and financial resources. Here our altruistic impulses come into play. We find fulfilment in striving to make the world a better place for everyone. We can take up the reins of the human evolutionary process, and as we drive along, allow our curiosity free scope to ponder the mystery of it all. Existence is inexplicable. Science provides some enlightenment, but the mystery remains. There is certainly no solution to be found in a cosmic fairy, only much painful brooding over the workings and outcome of the cosmic design: how can innocent suffering be so widespread and what lies in store for us in the "life" to come?

Let us embrace the rational attitude of humanism and make the most of the only life we can know.

Postscript 4

We must ask how successful we have been in communicating what humanism is all about. We have written for thinking people, but if we have caused offence by failing to produce a scholarly work, free from incoherences and what philosophers call "non-sequitors" (unjustified conclusions), we ask readers to pause before condemning us.

When apes developed calls that denoted the presence of specific predators, identifying leopards, snakes or eagles, they imparted information essential to their survival. Language followed and, together with social instincts that humans have gradually acquired, became the life-blood of civilisation.

This condensed survey continues with the invention of writing, printing and now the sophisticated information technology embodied in computers and the internet. So we might have supposed that it has now been made possible to communicate all that we know. But it need not be so. False or misleading ideas can spread, as Richard Dawkins expresses it, like viruses. To gain immunity we need the clear thinking that education can provide.

This book has presented humanism as a new challenge based on a Darwinian interpretation of human nature. We are entirely part of nature and are seriously deceived if we suppose that there is any non-human or supernatural presence – some cosmic fairy – that envelops us. So when we consider the human ability to communicate, we are looking at an exclusively human phenomenon. Untold confusion has arisen from the notion that there is some omniscient God who knows what is best for us, and has planned our lives and revealed his will to chosen religious professionals. In Chapter 1 we raised the problem of a divine language. It has never been sorted out or even admitted. But it is no mere frivolous quibble. How did God speak to himself before the advent of human tongues? This is a fair question for religious people who have invented God in a human image.

So we face the mystery of existence; but we have social instincts and if we co-operate on human terms, we can take charge of our future evolution and find a way of making life on earth more worthwhile for all who live there.

Since its emergence on this planet, life has covered much ground to produce the evolution of human beings. Inadequate though our words may have been, the communication embodied in history itself speaks of progress and supports our hope that humanists need not despair of the future. That the "Darwinian Enlightenment" is the basis of our optimism may surprise those professional philosophers who have not realised its relevance. This, however, has been our main theme. We have addressed thoughtful laymen, but should the book fall into the hands of the philosophers or their students, let them take heed of what Darwin can teach us. They show little sign of doing so. This is made plain in a book by the American philosopher, Daniel C. Dennett, entitled *Darwin's Dangerous Idea* (published by Allen Lane in 1995). He spends over 500 pages describing "evolution and the meanings of life", but does not seem concerned about the problem of God's intelligence. (He regards Darwin's idea as dangerous because it has disturbed many philosophers and some scientists – such as Paul Davies – who are loath to see purpose excluded from the universe.) The Enlightenment of the 17th and 18th centuries centered around the nature and works of man; the "Darwinian Enlightenment" has shown up the nature of God, revealing him as a "Cosmic Fairy", the product of human imagination. Humanism thus inspires a motivation that far surpasses anything to be found in the make-belief of religion. It encourages us to think: to wake up to the fact that we have evolved social instincts. Let us cultivate them. Therein lies our hope and the challenge of humanism. The future is up to us, not to the imaginary God disposed of by Darwin's idea. As the third Millennium approaches, we hope that civilisation will survive and flourish. "New waves of Darwinian thinking", to quote Daniel Dennett, will be needed to bring this about.

EPILOGUE

I hoed and trenched and weeded,
    And took the flowers to fair:
I brought them home unheeded;
    The hue was not the wear.

So up and down I sow them
    For lads like me to find,
When I shall lie below them,
    A dead man out of mind.

Some seed the birds devour,
    And some the season mars,
But here and there will flower
    The solitary stars,

And fields will yearly bear them
    As light-leaved spring comes on,
And luckless lads will wear them
    When I am dead and gone.

Our discussion of humanism has affirmed an attitude of hope, so why conclude with an epilogue featuring Housman's seemingly pessimistic poem?

While sowing the seeds of humanism, we have cherished the expectation that readers who have patiently walked with us all the way, will be stirred by a vision of the whole humanist landscape. For the resulting stars will not flower in solitude, but reveal the fascinating richness, variety and beauty that the world can provide. This is what humanism does for us.

We have quoted Housman's verses (the last poem in "The Shropshire Lad") to depict a sad contrast. Many sensitive people are dissatisfied by the make-believe of religion, and still seek something credible. In humanism we enter a real garden, where the sights and scents are not illusory. Natural processes have inexplicably placed us in a potential paradise. Let friendship sustain us in the face of the mystery of existence.

136

INDEX

Adam and Eve   105
Agnosticism   2, 27
Alexander the Great   76f
Altruism   23, 107, 169, 133
Atheism   2, 27
Attenborough, Sir David   131
Arnold, Matthew   128
Astrology   90f
Augustine, St.   24, 110

Bacon, Francis   42
Bellamy, David   131
Bereavement   22, 126
Bible   39f
Big Bang theory   47
Biology   79
Bowker, John   94
Brain   58, 65, 67
Brook, Rupert, "Heaven"   89–90
Browning, Robert   196
Butler, Samuel   31

Conscience   32
Consciousness   3f, 64f, 125
Cicero, Marcus Tullius   31, 103
Clark, Sir Kenneth (Lord Clark)
   35ff
Civilisation   35ff, 39
Chance   54
Crusades   104
Cupitt, Don   128
Christianity
   A superior ethic   42
   Answer to death   14f
   Believers' attitudes to   20
   Christianity and morality
      29f

Christianity and prayer   24
Contradictory dogmas   9
Emotional attitude   8
Final truth   47
Reviewed in New Testament
   102ff
Views of Church of England
   bishops   93
Crusades   104

Darwin, Charles   1ff, 112, 134
   Origin of Species   12
Dark Ages   35
Dawkins, Richard   134
Davies, Prof. Paul   109ff
Death   14f, 112
Descartes, René   60, 115
Deism   38
Democracy   44, 118
Dennett, Daniel C.
   "Darwin's Dangerous Idea"   134
Determinism   52ff
Devil   6
Dinosaurs   3ff
Dualism   45, 58

Education   71ff, 78f, 107
Einstein, Albert   110
Emotion   8ff, 82ff
Emperor's New Clothes   45
Epicurus   86
Erasmus, Desiderius   36
Evolution   1f, 4, 33, 79

Fairies   2, 27
Faith   8, 43
Family   80

Feelings 9f
Freedom 53ff
French language 69f
Freud 38
Friendship 36, 56, 81, 83
Garden of Eden 3
Genesis 47, 116
God
    Activity 3f
    Anthropomorphism 46
    As defined by Prof. Davies
        109
    Attitude to dinosaurs 5
    Belief unnecessary? 30
    Correct approach to 11
    Divine nature 9, 47, 63, 93,
        101, 104, 118f, 121ff, 125f,
        132, 134f
    Emotional need 24ff
    Existence of 2ff
    Explanation of the universe
        25
    God and atheism 27
    God and creation 1ff
    God and human choice 53
    God and salvation 49
    God and sin 29f
    God and suffering 16f
    God in poetry 89f
    Intimacy with God 20
    Invention of the Devil 6
    Life without God 41
    Reality of God 116
    Searching for God 84f
    Theism and deism 38f
Greek civilisation 76
Greek philosophers 86

Happiness 16f, 18, 20f, 80, 130
Hell 103
History 76
Hobbies 78f
Hope 33, 43, 79, 133
Humanism
    Answer to death 14ff, 115
    Approach to humanism 13,
        28
    Books on humanism 130

Challenges of humanism 50,
    124
Claims can be tested 65
Definition 125
Derived from Darwin 112
Dispels anxiety 88
Humanism and politics
    117f
Inspiration of humanism
    132
Intellectual gift 20f
Mental liberation 57
Merits of humanism 5ff, 107
Nature of humanism 85, 101
Not a religion 34
Practical implications 41f
Relation to psychology 70
Secures the future 33
Simplicity 10f
Humanist organisations 129
Housman, A.E. 103

Infinity 47, 121
Intelligence 3ff, 48, 131
Inquisition 104

Jesus 103

Knight, Margaret, *Honest to Man*
    102ff

Lamb, Charles 37
Language 4, 15, 26, 35, 133f
Learnardo da Vinci 12
Liberal education 79f, 81
Luther, Martin 36

Magicians 11
Materialism 19f, 52, 116
Mendel, Gregor 1
Mind 58ff, 63ff
Morality 30ff, 53, 75
More, Sir Thomas 36
Montaigne, Michel Eyquem de 36f
Mysticism 47

Nature Study 78
New Testament 102ff

Newton, Sir Isaac   12, 38, 101, 109f

Old Testament   106ff
Open society   51, 57
Origin of the universe   47

Pascal, Blaise   6
Paul, St.   34, 83
Peacock, Arthur   98
Pericles   86
Play   74f
Polkinghorne, John   98
Prayer   24
Progress   33, 134
Protagorus   86
Providence   47
Psychology   58ff, 62f, 70, 120
Purpose   46ff
Quakers   105

Reason and emotion   82ff
Religion
    Clash with science   11f
    Conflicting doctrines   9
    Definition   34
    Devisive doctrines   42f
    Emotional influences   8
    Influence continues   116f
    Intolerance   19
    Religion and morality   29f
    Survival assets   25ff
    Takes over in a crisis   14
    Threatened by Darwin   1f
Renaissance   21, 37f
Renaissance Humanism   35ff
Robinson, Dr. John   102

Royal Society   12
Ruskin, John   121
Ryle, Gilbert   59ff

Science   11, 22
Science fiction   47
Samaritan, the Good   54
Scott, Capt. Robert   79
Scott, Sir Peter   79
Self discipline   73, 75, 77
Self consciousness   4, 14, 44, 64f, 91f
Sex   105
Sensation   18f, 22f
Shakespeare, William   27, 36f
Sin   29f, 53, 71, 77, 105
Slavery   105
Soul   60f, 120
Spiritual   20f, 35
Spiritualism   19
Spirits and fairies   5, 127
Suffering   16
Superstition   118

Templeton Prize   108
Theism   38
Theology   38
Truth   11

Victorian poets   87ff
Virgin birth   105f

Wilberforce, Bishop William   12
Will-power   54
Witch-hunting   104
Wolpert, Lewis   128